UNDERSTANDING SOCIAL NETWORKS

SAGE HUMAN SERVICES GUIDES, VOLUME 32

SAGE HUMAN SERVICES GUIDES

a series of books edited by ARMAND LAUFFER and published in cooperation with the University of Michigan School of Social Work.

1: **GRANTSMANSHIP** by Armand Lauffer with Milan Dluhy, William Lawrence, and Eloise Snyder
2: **CREATING GROUPS** by Harvey J. Bertcher and Frank F. Maple
3: **UNDERSTANDING YOUR SOCIAL AGENCY** by Armand Lauffer, Lynn Nybell, Carla Overberger, Beth Reed, and Lawrence Zeff
4: **SHARED DECISION MAKING** by Frank F. Maple
5: **VOLUNTEERS** by Armand Lauffer and Sarah Gorodezky with Jay Callahan and Carla Overberger
6: **RESOURCES** by Armand Lauffer with Bonnie Carlson, Kayla Conrad, and Lynn Nybell
7: **FINDING FAMILIES** by Ann Hartman
8: **NO CHILD IS UNADOPTABLE** edited by Sallie R. Churchill, Bonnie Carlson, and Lynn Nybell
9: **HEALTH NEEDS OF CHILDREN** by Roger Manela and Armand Lauffer with Eugene Feingold and Ruben Meyer
10: **GROUP PARTICIPATION** by Harvey J. Bertcher
11: **BE ASSERTIVE** by Susan Stone Sundel and Martin Sundel
12: **CHILDREN IN CRISIS** by Carmie Thrasher Cochrane and David Voit Myers
13: **COMMUNICATION IN THE HUMAN SERVICES** by Marcia S. Joslyn-Scherer
14: **NEEDS ASSESSMENT** by Keith A. Neuber with William T. Atkins, James A. Jacobson, and Nicholas A. Reuterman
15: **DEVELOPING CASEWORK SKILLS** by James A. Pippin
16: **MUTUAL HELP GROUPS** by Phyllis R. Silverman
17: **EFFECTIVE MEETINGS** by John E. Tropman
18: **AGENCY AND COMPANY** by Louis A. Ferman, Roger Manela, and David Rogers
19: **USING MICROCOMPUTERS IN SOCIAL AGENCIES** by James B. Taylor
20: **CHANGING ORGANIZATIONS AND COMMUNITY PROGRAMS** by Jack Rothman, John L. Erlich, and Joseph G. Teresa
21: **MATCHING CLIENTS AND SERVICES** by R. Mark Mathews and Stephen B. Fawcett
22: **WORKING WITH CHILDREN** by Dana K. Lewis
23: **MAKING DESEGREGATION WORK** by Mark A. Chesler, Bunyan I. Brant, and James E. Crowfoot
24: **CHANGING THE SYSTEM** by Milan J. Dluhy
25: **HELPING WOMEN COPE WITH GRIEF** by Phyllis R. Silverman
26: **GETTING THE RESOURCES YOU NEED** by Armand Lauffer
27: **ORGANIZING FOR COMMUNITY ACTION** by Steve Burghardt
28: **AGENCIES WORKING TOGETHER** by Robert J. Rossi, Kevin J. Gilmartin, and Charles W. Dayton
29: **EVALUATING YOUR AGENCY'S PROGRAMS** by Michael J. Austin, Gary Cox, Naomi Gottlieb, J. David Hawkins, Jean M. Kruzich, and Ronald Rauch
30: **ASSESSMENT TOOLS** by Armand Lauffer
31: **UNDERSTANDING PROGRAM EVALUATION** by Leonard Rutman and George Mowbray
32: **UNDERSTANDING SOCIAL NETWORKS** by Lambert Maguire
33: **FAMILY ASSESSMENT** by Adele M. Holman

A **SAGE** HUMAN SERVICES GUIDE **32**

UNDERSTANDING SOCIAL NETWORKS

Lambert MAGUIRE

Published in cooperation with the University of
Michigan School of Social Work

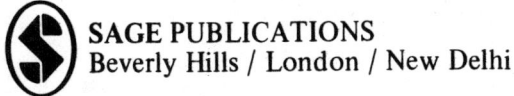
SAGE PUBLICATIONS
Beverly Hills / London / New Delhi

Copyright © 1983 by Sage Publications, Inc.

All rights reserved. No part of this book may be reproduced or utilized in any form or by any means, electronic or mechanical, including photocopying, recording, or by any information storage and retrieval system, without permission in writing from the publisher.

For information address:

SAGE Publications, Inc.
275 South Beverly Drive
Beverly Hills, California 90212

SAGE Publications India Pvt. Ltd.
C-236 Defence Colony
New Delhi 110 024, India

SAGE Publications Ltd
28 Banner Street
London EC1Y 8QE, England

Printed in the United States of America

Library of Congress Cataloging in Publication Data

Maguire, Lambert.
   Understanding social networks.

   (Sage human services guides ; v. 32)
   "Published in cooperation with the University of Michigan School of Social Work."
   1. Social structure. 2. Interpersonal relations. 3. Self-help groups. 4. Social service. I. University of Michigan. School of Social Work. II. Title. III. Series.
HM131.M3195   1983   305   83-4489
ISBN 0-8039-2010-5 (pbk.)

FIRST PRINTING

CONTENTS

Introduction		7
PART I	Networking: What It Is and Why We Do It	
Chapter 1	What Is Networking?	13
Chapter 2	Networking and Self-Help	27
Chapter 3	Social Networks and Social Support	43
PART II	Networking: The Interventions	
Chapter 4	Networking with Individuals	63
Chapter 5	Self-Help Groups	83
Chapter 6	Networking with Organizations	97
Chapter 7	Networking with Communities	111
About the Author		119

INTRODUCTION

New and innovative approaches are needed to meet the needs of the public. Networking approaches that maximize the use of natural helping networks and that use professionals more efficiently must be developed and tested. This book is a step in that direction.

This book is organized so that the reader will learn what networks are, which research supports their use, and how to organize supportive and helpful networks around individuals, self-help groups, communities, and organizations for the purposes of support, treatment, prevention, rehabilitation, advocacy, or simply improved communication and understanding. It is oriented toward a diverse audience, including practitioners and students in the mental health and social services professions.

Network strategies generally refer to a wide range of developing, revised, as well as quite old interventions that attempt to link people up with their own actual or potential social networks. This requires both multiple linkages and chain reactions. Individual networking requires that one link a person up with his or her friends, relatives, neighbors, or whoever else may be in a position to help, but also that the members of the network that one helps to find and develop will affect each other in some positive way. Networkers set up multiple linkages and then facilitate or help establish chain reactions. For the most part, their strategies rely on natural, informal, or nonprofessional support systems of helpers to serve as the network. However, in some strategies, such as networking with organizations or to a lesser extent within communities, the natural network members will consist of professionals.

Mental health, social service, and other helping professionals have been subject to a wide variety of fads and trends over the years, some of which have been nonproductive. The need that people have in our modern society to deal realistically with the everyday social and emotional problems that we all have has supported the development of many untried and untested strategies. Some have helped, some have hurt, and some have simply not affected people.

There is always the danger that networking strategies could indeed be developed and perceived as a mere fad and thus discarded before being adequately tested, a possibility that we shall treat thoroughly and directly. For this reason, the book is divided into two parts. Part I consists of three chapters and establishes in both theory and practice the foundation for network interventions. Chapter 1 explains what networking is and gives examples of it, as well as establishing it in its historical context. Networking is not seen as anything particularly new or radical, but rather as an amalgam of approaches, variations of which have been used since people first crawled out of the caves and defended themselves against prehistoric beasts. It also shows the reader how to map his or her own personal network.

Chapter 2 discusses networking as a means of self-help and explains why it is being scrutinized at present. Several reasons are cited for this current interest. These include general disenchantment with professionals and experts, the rise in the self-help and mutual aid movement because of its own success, and the fact that we now know more clearly when and how professionals can work together with networks. Chapter 3 examines the problems of the present mental health and social service system, as well as some contemporary purposes of network analysis and how networks can affect health and mental health. All of these factors are related to the need to make our services more efficient and effective by purposefully using and directing various types of networks that already exist or that could be easily developed.

Part II examines in detail various strategies applicable to individuals (Chapter 4), self-help or mutual aid groups (Chapter 5), organizations (Chapter 6), and communities (Chapter 7), rather than relying solely on professionals doing the interventions directly. The common thread in each of these strategies is that they all involve multiple connections and chain reactions, and that the networker serves as a linking agent and facilitator of the second-order, or indirect, links. In other words, each network strategy defines a unit of intervention (an individual, family, or group), establishes ways to connect that unit to its appropriate social or natural helping network, and then examines ways to support the connections or links among the network members.

In Chapter 4, for instance, the reader will learn not only how to analyze a personal network, but also how to network for the purposes of linking a person up with the appropriate members to help with a variety of material resources, with a job, or, in some circumstances, with therapeutic support.

Chapter 5 looks at self-help and mutual aid groups and explains two ways of working with such groups as a networker. In one method, the networker develops a clearinghouse, pulls together information about groups in the area, and gets them to form a network of self-help groups. In the other method, he or she becomes a developer or facilitator for the members themselves, who actually do most of the direct organizing of the groups.

Chapter 6 looks at ways in which one can network with organizations. These include case management (pooling professional contacts and resources for a particular case), or can include developing a human service network. A human service network is an ongoing committee of leaders of human service organizations who meet regularly to share resources and work out community problems.

Chapter 7 considers various means of working with natural helping networks in communities, as well as other ways of developing a community's resources for the purpose of empowerment. It cannot be read in isolation because it relies heavily on strategies used in the previous chapters.

The networkers who actually carry out a strategy are usually mental health, social service, or some other sort of helping professionals, although there are numerous examples of natural helpers, such as volunteers and community leaders, who also serve this function. The people helped include those traditionally aided by the helping professions; that is, those with definable social, emotional, and interpersonal problems that they cannot solve alone. Most networking strategies are not therapy and, although they are certainly therapeutic at times, they are really just a way of getting by with a little help from our friends.

Part I

NETWORKING: WHAT IT IS AND WHY WE DO IT

Chapter 1

WHAT IS NETWORKING?

"Networking" is a term that has been used and abused a great deal in recent years. Because it has been used to describe so many different processes and approaches, its actual meaning and thus its potential utility to helpers and/or practitioners can be severely diminished before it has really had a chance to be understood and tried. In this chapter we will cover not only what the term means, but also what it does not mean. In general terms, networking can be defined as a purposeful process of linking three or more people together and of establishing connections and chain reactions among them. It is not a new process or technique. In fact, it has been with us throughout history and is only now becoming more focused and efficient as research is developed in the field and as new networking strategies are developed and tested by mental health, social service, and health practitioners, as well as concerned community leaders.

Practitioners can no longer afford to continue doing what they have always done, with limited results, nor can they experiment with new strategies that have no basis in research. Many networking approaches have immense potential, but this potential could be sidetracked and the entire process rejected if practitioners are not aware of the research already conducted in psychology, anthropology, sociology, public health, and epidemiology, and of the results that either support or refute networking strategies.

Networks are defined in many ways. Mitchell (1969: 2) defines a social network as a "specific set of linkages among a defined set of persons with the additional property that the characteristics of their linkage as a whole may be used to interpret the social behavior of the persons involved." Anthropologist J. A. Barnes (1972: 43) defines networks on the basis of their analytical capabilities, describing them as "a set of points which are joined by lines; the points of the image are people or sometimes groups and the lines indicate which people interact with each other." Finally, Walker et al. (1977: 35) see social networks as "that set of personal contacts through which the individual maintains his social identity and receives emotional support, material aid and services, information, and new social contacts." Other social scientists use the term in either of two ways. Some use it metaphorically, referring most often to a general network of social relations, while the term "social network" is usually reserved for analytical scientists who use many developing, mathematically based approaches for measuring, graphing, and statistically defining the social bonds, causal connections, and interrelationships within networks (Barnes, 1972).

Networks can be analyzed in depth using a wide variety of techniques and analytical variables (Barnes, 1972; Boissevain and Mitchell, 1973; Fischer et al., 1977; Mitchell, 1969). Some of the more commonly used critical dimensions of dyadic or two-person links in a network include *multiplexity,* or the number of roles or relations (for example, brother, neighbor, and co-worker) that connect two people; *symmetry,* or the balance of power or profit; and *intensity,* or the degree of commitment in a link. Other dimensions of the entire network and its sets of links can also be described. For instance, *range,* which refers to the number of actors connected in a link; *density,* or the extent of interlinkage among the actors (usually expressed as the ratio of the number of existing links to the number of possible links); *reachability,* or the average number of links needed to connect any two actors to the shortest route; and *clustering,* or the extent to which the total network is divided into distinguishable cliques.

Let us try out a few of these terms. In describing the link between a man and his brother who lives next door, one could say that in relation to multiplexity, the link is supported by two roles. If one brother has more resources (personal or financial) or more status, then the link is asymmetrical, and the intensity or degree of commitment can either be measured as a function of how much or little the brothers indicate caring for one another, or on the basis of the types of services or assistance they will provide each other. These links can be statistically defined and measured, as well as graphically displayed using lines and paths. The purpose of such analyses is to examine in detail the relationships people have between and among themselves so that the causes and effects of such relationships can be better understood. If one were to examine the larger network of which these brothers are a part, one might choose to include a sister who is personally closer to one brother than to another, and another neighbor, who never met the sister but knows of her from the brothers. If it were to be based on emotional attachment, this network might be diagrammed as in Figure 1.1, with brother "A" being the ego or central figure, "B" the other brother, "C" the sister, and "D" the neighbor to both "A" and "B."

Judging from the length of the lines between characters, it appears that "A" is more attached, or literally "closer," to his sister ("C") than his brother ("B"), and that "B" is more distant than "A" to their neighbor, "D." For each type of networking intervention, an example will be provided of at least one way to examine practically the appropriate type of network. The next section tells how to analyze a social network.

MAPPING A NETWORK

In order to get a clearer idea of what a network is, try mapping your own personal network in the following exercise, which was recommended to me by David Todd. Take a large piece of paper and draw five concentric circles, leaving enough space between each circle to do some writing. Now divide the circles into four wedge- or pie-shaped sections (see Figure 1.2). Label the sections for each of your major spheres of influence: family and relatives, friends, neighbors, colleagues from work or school, and professional caregivers.

The center circle is you—the ego, central figure, or anchor point of your network configuration. Beginning with the circle nearest to the center, write in the names or initials of those closest to you within each sphere of influence. In the first section closest to yourself may be your wife or husband, followed in the second section of that family sphere by your children, parents, and brothers or sisters. The next outlying sections or section may contain in-laws, cousins, aunts, uncles, grandparents, and so on. In this and other spheres, there will often be overlap. For instance, for most of us our friends will sometimes be our work colleagues or neighbors as well. Where possible, limit people to only one sphere. Once you have filled out all the concentric areas in all the spheres, connect the names of people who know each other with lines. This is your network.

If you have many lines between and among your network members, it is a dense network. If these linkages are infrequent, it is not dense. If you have direct cross-linkages between many members of different spheres of influence, you have a high degree of reachability within the network. The strength of one's network is sometimes assessed as how "close" the network members are to you at the anchor point.

For many, this is a fascinating, revealing, and sometimes surprising exercise. I have used it with a wide variety of audiences in workshops, classes, and conferences. My graduate students, who tend to be predominantly in their 20s, often note that changes in marital status and the presence or absence of children make a significant difference in their

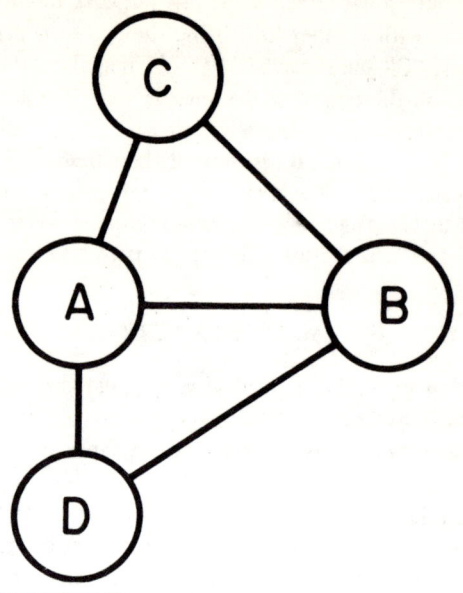

Figure 1.1

networks. For instance, young women who have been married for at least a couple of years tend to diagram their networks of friends as consisting largely of other young married couples. A few short years before, however, they would have had few if any close married friends. Likewise, the single students' friends are often other single students.

The married students, particularly the older ones, also recognize that their networks become further differentiated on the basis of whether their friends have children or not, a finding that is consistent with other research (Campbell et al., 1976) showing how networks are often established within one's neighborhood on the basis of friendships among children. Young married students with children frequently note that many of their friendships are with other couples who also have children, particularly if the children are of the same age and sex. Not infrequently, divorced students, both male and female, have commented that their network configuration changed after the divorce and that they reverted back to having many single or divorced friends, rather than married couples. If they maintained custody of the children, the link might be maintained with the same-sex parent, but it often became more distant and focused more on the child's needs. For some, this was a disturbing revelation.

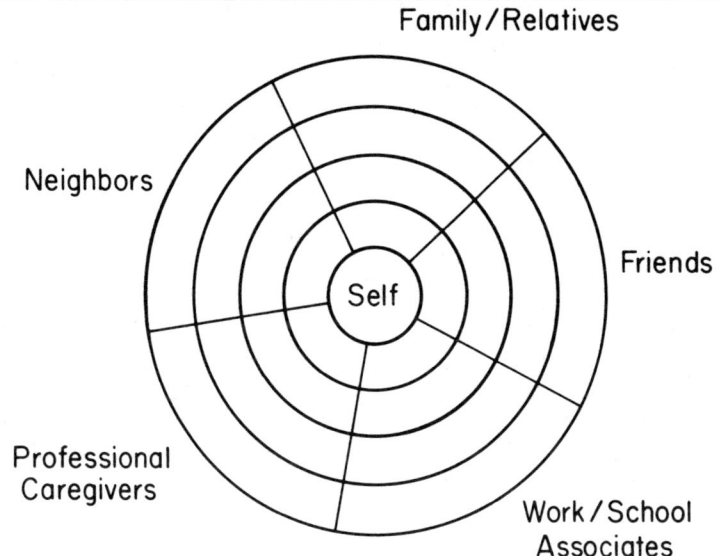

SOURCE: Todd, D. "Appendix: Social Network Mapping," in W. R. Curtis, The Future Use of Social Networks in Mental Health. Boston: Social Matrix Research, Inc., 1979. Reprinted by permission.

Figure 1.2: Mapping One's Social Network

Participants in conferences where I have used the exercise sometimes note with surprise the high degree of homogeneity among their network of friends in terms of education, income, age, and interests. This is sometimes a shock to white, middle-class liberal professionals who are forced to recognize that their inner circle of friends rarely includes people of different races or social backgrounds.

Several other, rather clear patterns emerge from these networks. For instance, if people live in the same area for all of their lives, they are likely to have more multiplexity in role members because their closest friends are usually from their old childhood neighborhood as well. In some instances these network bonds are further strengthened by the fact that cousins, grandparents, aunts, and uncles all live in the neighborhood, and even those neighbors who are not directly related in many instances share the same ethnic, racial, or religious background. Thus it is not unusual, at least in older and more established cities such as Pittsburgh, Chicago, and New York, and in rural communities to see very dense networks of people. They are linked together on the basis of family and neighborhood ties, as well as work ties (for example, the family-owned grocery store, dry cleaning business, or construction/contracting company) that consist almost entirely of relatives.

THE OLD AND THE NEW:
BRINGING BACK FAMILY AND FRIENDS

The history of people helping people has little similarity to the highly specialized, professional system of today. In fact, the onset of professionalism in the fields of mental health and social services is a purely twentieth-century phenomenon. Before this century, people relied solely on friends, neighbors, and family to provide them with all of their emotional, social, and economic support. At the turn of this century, psychoanalysis and all other forms of psychotherapy were virtually unknown, and psychiatric hospitals were few and primitive. The Social Security Act was more than thirty years in the future, and the psychotropic wonder drugs of today could not even have been imagined. The fields of social work, public health, vocational guidance, counselor education, and rehabilitation therapy had not really begun, and specializations in community mental health, job finding for the handicapped, or such medical subspecialties as neonatology or hematology would have been similarly incomprehensible to even the most knowledgeable and imaginative of people living at that time. Furthermore, there was neither strong government influence nor any professional organizations to protect and defend their membership.

In 1900, a woman concerned about her child's behavior could only seek help from her mother or another relative or neighbor with children. The advisors she chose would have been picked on the basis of their knowledge about this sort of problem, their genuine concern about the woman and the child, and their ability to be helpful, based on past experience. In some instances, only one advisor was eventually chosen, and this person may well have helped many others with similar problems. This advisor was a specialist of sorts who knew "all about children" and was both able and willing to give advice, as well as direct help with the child. Sometimes the specialist might even have "referred" the mother and child to another specialist friend of hers who knew even more than she about this particular type of childhood problem. In fact, a network of what some now call lay specialists or natural helpers existed in nearly all communities and for nearly any problem related to children.

These specialists may have been retired or even active schoolteachers, parents, or grandparents who were respected for having raised their own children well, or simply people who understood children and knew how to deal with their problems. They often knew each other and were linked together by their common knowledge, interest, expertise, and willingness to help. It would not have been necessary for the mother to know all of the people in this network. As long as she knew one person in it, or even one person who knew another who was in it, the linkages and chain reactions could be set in place that would get her the help she needed. This was networking then, and it still is today.

Perhaps this turn-of-the-century family had a financial problem. In those days, when sexual roles were more traditionally and strictly defined, the husband or father would have assumed the responsibility for borrowing or earning the needed money or substantive resources. He may have asked a cousin to intercede for him in talking to the town's banker. The banker would have then gone out and asked other relatives and friends of the person if they thought the person was a good risk, and if they personally would help pay back the loan if he defaulted. Based on the banker's indirect knowledge of the man, and on his personal relationships with and trust in mutual friends or relatives of the man, the banker would make a decision as to whether or not the loan was a safe one. A contract or loan agreement may or may not have been signed, but repayment was guaranteed more by fear of future exclusion or ostracism from the community's financial as well as all other helping networks as it was from any legal or even financial fears. This was also networking.

This same hypothetical turn-of-the-century family would have had a circle of friends on whom they could rely for social support and help. Their friends probably shared some common interests or traits, such as the same ethnic background, religion, georgraphic location, education, age, or number of children. This socializing and friendship was not just with one family, but with several families who knew and liked each other, and who shared at least some of these commonalities. This, too, was networking.

Networking is as vital, important, and viable a process today as it was many years ago, but today there are many alternatives to it. The hypothetical woman at the turn of the century had relatively few options, and virtually none of them consisted of groups of expert or professional helpers. Today, the person seeking help for a child might just as likely be the father as the mother, and while the options still include parents, grandparents, neighbors, and other helpful, concerned advisors and lay specialists, they also include trained professionals.

Today's network is potentially far more efficient and effective because it includes social workers, as well as child psychiatrists and psychologists working in clinics with large support staffs, and a vast system of well-trained social service and mental health professionals. The financially troubled family of today may still have the cousin with banking connections, but if they do not have a networker or community leader to guide and support them in making that initial connection, who will in turn link up with the banking officials, they will find it hard to get a loan.

Finally, the turn-of-the-century family's circle of friends would be little different from today's, at least in terms of purpose. This purpose is to talk over concerns, share common interests, and to relax and enjoy each other's company. This is as true today as it was then, and although there may not be quite so much of a tendency today for a network of friends to be homogeneous, one's network of closest friends remains surprisingly similar to oneself in their general characteristics (Fischer et al., 1977).

My own education in networking began after I left the University of Chicago and moved to the Pine Ridge Indian Reservation in South Dakota. Its people, the Dakota Sioux, had been described to me as an independent and rugged tribe of people. These descendants of Crazy Horse, who was central in the defeat of Custer, had themselves been cruelly defeated in a massacre some years later near the village of Wounded Knee. The pain of what the white man had done clearly lingered on, and their trust of white professionals was understandably guarded.

With the enthusiasm of all young recent graduates, however, I earnestly began developing my caseload. Even though much of my graduate training up to that point had been in group psychotherapy, I had been advised against forming groups with them because they supposedly did not open up or talk in groups. I also found that my psychoanalytically based treatment approach was of little use. The people I saw were either long-term patients who had been coming in previously for years to see other staff, primarily for the purpose of keeping them functioning and out of the state hospital, or they were individuals who were fairly transient and not well connected to the tribal members. This second group consisted primarily of Indians from other reservations, and mixed breeds who traveled among several reservations getting services where they could from various social service, welfare, or mental health programs.

Fortunately, my work also consisted of community organization activities, consultation with several schools and church groups, and the opportunity to teach courses at the tribe's community college. In fact, Wounded Knee was assigned to me as an area to be "organized." Although my caseload, with its two extremes, was not too satisfying—especially for one with a traditional psychoanalytic background—my other tasks became increasingly enjoyable and productive.

These people also eventually helped me to answer the questions that had been gnawing at me almost since I arrived on the reservation. Where were all the others who needed help? Where were those with marital problems, child-raising difficulties, and disorders related to depression, anxiety, and stress-related tension? Why was I seeing this relatively small caseload of people when I knew that there were many alcohol-related problems, as well as widespread family dysfunction? Finally, why was I accomplishing so little with some of the clients I saw? I knew from the professional local grapevine that my clients were also being helped at the welfare office, the hospital, and the Bureau of Indian Affairs. So why were we all doing so much for so few with such minimal results?

The answers to all these questions only became clear after I got to know the Indian community leaders and the various matriarchs and patriarchs of the major *tiyospayes* (the Sioux word for the extended family or kin network) on the reservation. As I lived on the reservation, socializing and developing relationships with people, it became apparent that the same sorts of family problems and psychiatric disorders did exist but were handled within networks of family and friends. This was also true of the political offices and jobs on the reservation. A handful of powerful tiyospayes, which ultimately linked most of the 11,000 Indian residents, took care of their own relatives. In fact, child-raising responsibilities were as much or even more the responsibility of grandparents as parents. Frequently aunts, uncles, and distant cousins all lived in the same household or, if in the country, in a cluster of homes, huts, trailers, and tents. Thus the household compositions were an anthropologist's nightmare—or dream—of familial patterns of interaction and responsibility. In fact, the Indian people often joked that their families consisted of grandparents, parents, five or more children, a few cousins, aunts and uncles, four or more dogs, and at least one anthropologist.

These families were all involved in networks of relatives, and even allied families (through intermarriage), that helped their individual members socially, emotionally, and behaviorally. Family gatherings, and particularly funerals, were large gatherings with a great deal of food and presents for everyone. Certain family members avoided other family members either because one family was "too white," or too rich, or too poor, or because great uncle John Red Shirt had been shot by one of the family members forty years ago.

Individuals would go to the matriarchs or, seemingly less often, to the patriarch of the tiyospayes and tell them their problems. This family head would then talk to another family member or two who was close to the situation, or who had a knowledge or history of that type of problem, and get them all involved in helping. Every tiyospaye was fiercely political, and the election of the tribal chief, which happened every two years, was a time of political horse-trading and backroom dealing that would have made Mayor Daley green with envy. Tribal and even federal jobs were traded for support in the upcoming elections, and the "in-town" mixed bloods fought it out politically with the full bloods, who tended to live in the countryside, on a regular basis. But these elections meant jobs, and jobs meant security in an area where both were scarce.

If an individual needed help, and he or she was a member of one of the larger, more powerful tiyospayes, a job, financial resources, as well as good council and advice could be offered. Given the tremendous power of the kin network in that culture, even marital problems could be resolved by the tiyospaye. I was familiar with one case where a married man and father of four was having an affair with a very young woman. After the wife finally got up the nerve to talk to her grandmother, who headed the tiyospaye, the matter was quickly resolved. Within a week the girl had been moved to the country to live with her rather strict aunt, the husband had been visited by his parents, who informed him that they were "disappointed," and the wife had accepted an offer from her two sisters to relieve her on a regular basis with child care and housecleaning responsibilities. In addition, one of the tribal policemen, who happened to be in the grandmother's tiyospaye, dropped by the husband's place of work to tell him that he would be arrested if he were found any evening without his wife. Finally, his employer at a federal agency told him to change his ways or be fired. The man changed his ways.

Not all such networks help individuals. One town and surrounding area that were quite remote from the reservation's capital were virtually ruled by the matriarch of a very large, well-connected tiyospaye. Her son, who had been overly protected throughout his life, would terrorize other villagers. The area rarely had any police protection since the last two tribal police had been forced out of the area by this woman and her family, and her connections within the tribe as well as with the state and federal agencies made her and her son impervious to any local authority. While this woman's influence had been the dominant factor in the location of a large health clinic and school complex in that remote and sparsely populated part of the reservation, it had also been her influence that kept the clinic from being staffed properly (thus excluding any doctors, dentists, or nurses) and the school from being adequately operated. Her son, who once forced a school bus loaded with terrified children into a ditch near a highway with no consequences to himself, was an individual for whom help from the network had ultimately been a great disservice, both to himself and others.

HISTORY AND RECENT DEVELOPMENTS

The process of networking that involves professionals working with "helping networks" has been with us in this country for many years (Froland et al., 1981). There is a great deal of evidence that friends and neighbors, and relatives, help each other (Kulka et al., 1979; Campbell et al., 1976), volunteer their services for the sake of the community (Allen et al., 1980), support each other in groups against a common threat or problem (Silverman, 1980; Gartner and Riessman, 1981; Caplan and

Killilea, 1976), and network as community members to develop and protect their communities (Warren, 1981; Biegel and Naperstek, 1982). Networking is not only not dead, it is alive and well!

Social work history gives evidence of a strong networking tradition (Collins and Pancoast, 1976). At the turn of the century, when the field was beginning and masses of immigrants were arriving on America's shores, social workers used networking extensively. They helped to link up the new arrivals with others from their former homeland and frequently tried, before their arrival, to locate friends and relatives who knew them. Irish, Polish, and Italian priests, as well as German and Swedish ministers and rabbis from all over Europe, were brought into this process very successfully. The networking that was performed by professionals through charitable agencies, settlement houses, and churches no doubt contributed to the amazing advances of this country at that time and in subsequent years. Without that networking and people "taking care of their own," though with the frequent aid of professionals, the history of this country could have been quite different, as the poor and starving stagnated or even rebelled at the various ports of entry.

Networking is not new, it is simply improved. Years ago it was a "hit or miss" process. One either had friends and relatives and the prerequisite relationships and personality characteristics necessary to make the linkages, or one did not. Many did not. One either had the skills to ask the right people for the right resources in the right way at the right time, or one did not. Many did not.

Today, people whose relationships or linkages with potentially helpful family and friends are tenuous can be tremendously helped by an informed networker. The social network analyses that allow us to define clearly who should be involved in the helping network, as well as what that person can provide and when it should be provided, are all available. By learning how to analyze a network, help make connections, and support constructive chain reactions, one need not leave to chance what must be done.

Networking, however, is no replacement for professional services, nor can it be done by simply leaving people alone. The naive, simplistic, and many feel, vindictive, beliefs among many politicians who periodically slash away at federal, state, and local budgets will no doubt effect tremendous harm. The "good old days" were in fact quite bad for those who were isolated and/or unwilling or unable to make the necessary and appropriate linkages. Now those linkages can be made more efficiently and effectively, but there are skills and techniques that must be learned. These skills start with understanding how to analyze a network. A few practical examples of social network instruments are described in this book in Figures 1.2 and 4.4.

The development of network analysis has been of very recent origin. While several earlier anthropologists made metaphorical referrals to networks long ago, it was not until Elizabeth Bott's (1957/1971) network analysis of London families and marital network patterns, and Barnes's (1954) first analyses of relationships in Norwegian fishing villages, that at least the field of anthropology began studying networks among the social sciences. Anthropology is the field that started with and is still leading the way among network supporters. However, it did not develop until the late 1960s and early 1970s, with Mitchell's (1969) *Social Networks in Urban Situations,* Barnes's (1972) *Social Networks,* and Boissevain and Mitchell's (1973) *Network Analysis: Studies in Human Interaction.*

Even in anthropology, network thinking is very new. In the comprehensive *Anthropology Today,* by Kroebler et al. (1953), networks are barely mentioned. Its rapid development in that social science seems to be based on four factors (Wolfe, 1978). These include the changes in social theory, ethnographic experience, mathematics, and data processing. In social theory, the network model of social systems developed logically over the past thirty years, partially because of the change in interest toward relations and toward an interest in process rather than form. In relation to the ethnographic experience, or to the long-standing tradition within anthropology to do direct fieldwork with people who value kin and family ties, Wolfe (1978) feels that such a tradition better prepared anthropologists than other social scientists for network analyses. While sociologists and psychologists have more often relied on survey methods, which do not lend themselves particularly to developing rapport or even to obtaining entree into a system, the ethnographic experience deliberately uses those factors which other social scientists would in fact consider research contaminants.

The ethnographic experience makes deliberate use of all possible kinship and friendship connections, whereas the social survey method tends to "force one to leap from one subject (person) to another, each randomly chosen, or, worse still, deliberately chosen *because* the one has no relation to the other and is not thus 'contaminated' " (Wolfe, 1978: 57). Modern social network analysts seem to appreciate the sensitivity of the ethnographic approach, while still retaining the precision and depth allowed by the social survey approach.

The third factor in anthropology that has led to the current concern over networking is, interestingly enough, mathematics. By measuring and defining network terms such as connectedness, density, range, and centrality, mathematics not only clarifies the nature and functions of networks, but has developed the capacity to compare and contrast them with precision. By using graph theory, topology, and matrix algebra, whole new analytical dimensions for understanding patterns of relationships within networks have been developed. Thus, within the traditional anthropological approach, the communicational patterns and spheres of influence of the extended family networks of London can be compared with those of Norway, and African villages can be studied with a level of precision and analytical sophistication that was previously nonexistent. Of even more importance to practitioners in the fields of mental health and social services is the fact that this analytical capability can also be used to evaluate the functional potential of a variety of networks.

Finally, the technology of data processing has significantly increased our capacity to examine relationships, and thus, networks. Due to the fact that the number of linkages within networks increases almost exponentially with each new member, the problems of analyzing these complex relationships become incomprehensible, or at least complex, relatively quickly as the size of the network increases and/or the number of variables increases. Our boundaries in this particular area are now limited only by our capabilities to digest and understand what computers can deliver.

SUMMARY

Networking is a purposeful process of linking three or more people together while establishing connections and chain reactions among them. Before a networker can effectively and efficiently make those connections and encourage useful chain reactions, he or she must analyze the network.

Networking is an old process that has been used throughout the ages. However, some services that at one time belonged to family and friends alone are now performed by social workers and other professionals. This book will help the reader to explore ways of reconnecting with valuable social, family or community networks.

REFERENCES

ALLEN, K. K., J. L. DUTTON, G. MANSEN, L. J. PETERSON, and W. D. RYDBERG (1980) The Shape of Things to Come, 1980-1990: A Report from the National Forum on Volunteerism. Washington, DC: The National Center for Citizen Involvement.
BARNES, J. A. (1972) Social Networks. Reading, MA: Addison-Wesley.
―――― (1954) "Class and committees in a Norwegian island parish." Human Relations 7(1): 39-58.
BIEGEL, D. and A. NAPERSTEK [Eds.] (1982) Community Support Systems and Mental Health: Practice, Policy and Research. New York: Springer.

BOISSEVAIN, J. and J. C. MITCHELL [Eds.] Network Analysis: Studies in Human Interaction. The Hague: Mouton.

BOTT, E. (1957/1971) Family and Social Networks (2nd ed.). London: Tavistock.

CAMPBELL, A., D. E. CONVERSE, and W. L. RODGERS (1976) The Quality of American Life: SSA Edition. Ann Arbor, MI: Institute for Social Research.

CAPLAN, G. and M. KILLILEA [Eds.] (1976) Support Systems and Mutual Help. New York: Grune & Stratton.

COLLINS, A. H. and D. L. PANCOAST (1976) Natural Helping Networks. Washington, DC: National Association of Social Workers.

FISCHER, C., R. JACKSON, C. STUEVE, K. GERSON, and L. JONES (1977) Networks and Places. New York: Free Press.

FROLAND, C. D., L. PANCOAST, N. J. CHAPMAN, and P. J. KIMBOKO (1981) Helping Networks and Human Services. Beverly Hills, CA: Sage.

GARTNER, A. and F. RIESSMAN (1981) Help: A Working Guide to Self-Help Groups. New York: New Viewpoint Books.

KROEBLER, A. K. et al. (1953) Anthropology Today: An Encyclopedic Inventory. Chicago: University of Chicago Press.

KULKA, R., J. VEROFF, and E. DOUVAN (1979) "Social class and the rise of professional help for personal problems: 1957 and 1976." Journal of Health and Social Behavior 20: 2-17.

MITCHELL, J. C. [Ed.] (1969) Social Networks in Urban Situations. Manchester, Eng.: Manchester University Press.

SILVERMAN, P. (1980) Mutual Help Groups: Organization and Development. Beverly Hills, CA: Sage.

WALKER, K. N., A. MacBRIDE, and M.H.S. VACHON (1977) "Social support networks and the crisis of bereavement." Social Science and Medicine 2: 35-41.

WARREN, D. (1981) Helping Networks: How People Cope with Problems in the Urban Community. Notre Dame, IN: University of Notre Dame Press.

WOLFE, A. A. (1978) "The use of network thinking in anthropology." Social Networks 1(1): 53-64.

Chapter 2

NETWORKING AND SELF-HELP

THE RISE OF NETWORKING AND SELF-HELP

The formal system of helping is composed of social workers, psychologists, psychiatrists, nurses, counselors, doctors, and therapists of various sorts. The informal system is composed of relatives, friends, neighbors, and colleagues from work who help individuals who are willing and able to help themselves. The informal system is composed of "natural helpers" who differ from those who compose the formal system in that they are not professionally trained as helpers, they accept no pay, and they work out of their homes or, if they help at their places of employment, the type of help is not seen as a necessary part of the job. Furthermore, they often have a personal concern, relationship, or something in common with the person helped, and they may have a natural capacity to listen, advise, and act in a helping role. They do not have to establish a separate role as a helper, as professionals do, but rather tend to act naturally, spontaneously offering themselves as resources for self-help.

It is easy to idealize such people, since the description given is essentially that of a saint or at least an altruistic, concerned, and effective person whose primary goal is the betterment of others. However, they cannot provide many of the specialized services offered in the formal sector by professionals, nor is it fair to presume that many of those same altruistic and genuine qualities are not shared by professionals. People should go to professionals for services that require highly skilled and/or technical knowledge or capabilities, and to the informal sector for problems that require time and personal concern.

Both of these systems require networking. In fact, not only the same process is involved when networking in either a formal or an informal system, but often many of the same people as well. The problem in the past has been insufficient knowledge of the capabilities of the two systems on the part of those involved, as well as a certain degree of distrust. Until recent years, the training of professionals to work in the areas of mental health and social services had focused on the classical Freudian position of family and friends as factors in the development of psychopathology or other serious emotional problems. Their strengths and positive aspects, let alone their potential capabilities in alleviating problems, were rarely considered. Those in the informal or natural sector have generally felt reluctant to present themselves to professionals for help because they were afraid of stigmatizing themselves as being mentally ill or as having to get help from a counselor or social worker from public welfare, or even from a family service agency.

Networking strategies are supported at one extreme by those who say that such approaches can help nearly all people at all levels and essentially replace the formal systems of counseling, mental health, social services, or health care. Their argument is that the formal system has failed and is not capable of dealing with the vast and overwhelming problems of present-day individuals, so that alternatives that radically depart from the professional traditional services are needed. However, this argument is not supported by particularly strong empirical evidence. While there is a developing body of research indicating that the social support provided by networks of friends and relatives does provide help, it is not yet clear *how* they help. Although there is some research indicating that, in general, psychotherapy is essentially no more effective than leaving a person alone with no treatment (Gross, 1978), there are considerable methodological problems in drawing that conclusion.

Networking approaches are very promising when linked with other professional interventions. The traditional mental health and social services system, with its reliance on one-to-one, long-term services or treatment, leaves a great deal to be desired, but its detractors have too often discarded the good with the bad. In reality, some blending or increased understanding, communication, and mutual use of the two systems seem indicated. In the ensuing chapters of this book and in the strategies described, we will explore a more systematic, precise, and clearly defined blend of the best of the two systems. It is no longer sufficient just to drop the biases. Today, professionals must do more research in establishing the specifics of networking, while accepting nonprofessionals as partners and collaborators in the process.

There are many potential and actual reasons that we need to use networking strategies more fully. Since the government has been and will no doubt continue to be an erratic source of leadership and funding in the area of human services, a need has developed to stabilize and coordinate limited resources more effectively and to find and utilize natural human resources wherever they exist—which is essentially what networking is all about. As long as the formal system of human services relies on government funds for the bulk of its support, these services will continue to go through a regular "boom and bust" cycle. But the cost in human tragedies and misery is too high to continue in this manner. Minimally, a consistent core of dependable human resources, that is, people, services, and concrete supports such as money, food, and clothing must be made available. Since both the government and therefore the formal helping system are in a state of flux, the only consistent source is the natural network and support system. Networking strategies directed and coordinated by professionals but utilizing the natural networks to the utmost of their efficiency and effectiveness must serve as the foundation for future human services in good times as well as bad. A more consistent system based on a mutual respect and collaboration between the formal and informal helping systems will minimize the devastating effects of the political/economic purges that the government endures every few years, develop further the natural system, and bring people, groups, and communities closer to one another and to those who are most closely affected. Although this very general reason serves as the most immediate rationale for networking, there are many other specific reasons for practitioners to learn how to apply network strategies that maximize self-help resources.

First, there is an apparent disenchantment with professionals and experts, whether they are politicians, economists, child psychologists, or psychotherapists (Chu and Trotter, 1974; Gross, 1978). The public has come to realize that the professionals don't have all the answers. Second has been the success of the self-help movement in the areas of advocacy for causes or oppressed groups (Katz, 1982; Pollard, 1978) and in mutual help groups (Maguire, 1981; Gartner and Riessman, 1981; Lieberman and Borman, 1979; Silverman, 1980). Third, there are now at least four clearly defined instances where social workers can work together with self-help resources in order to maximize the strengths of both systems. This chapter will consider each of those issues.

Chapter 3 will deal with the research- and empirically based reasons for increased networking. These include, first of all, the perceived lack of dramatic outcomes—particularly in mental health (Garfield and Bergin,

1978), where longer-term, psychodynamically based approaches are still the mainstay, and in social services, where the vast health and welfare system is perceived as insensitive. The alternative of using people's own social networks or natural helping networks thus becomes viable. Another reason involves the recent advances in research methods, statistical procedures, and data analysis that have combined to give us a far greater capacity to examine not only the simple quantitative measures dealing with human interaction, but also qualitative assessments of how and why people develop friendships (Fischer et al., 1977) or go to certain friends or relatives, as opposed to others, for favors, support, help, or whatever.

This ability to analyze networks and their patterns of influence and communication can be very complex statistically (Barnes, 1972; Boissevain and Mitchell, 1973; Holland and Leinhardt, 1979; Wellman, 1981; Gottlieb, 1981). However, it can be used positively in clinical interventions by simply asking people some basic questions, which will be covered later. The fifth reason is the fact that a tremendous amount of epidemiological and social survey research indicates that supportive networks do serve as a general buffer against stress (Antonovsky, 1979), or as a correlate with a wide variety of health and mental health problems (President's Task Panel Reports, 1978; Caplan, 1974; Gottlieb, 1981; Nuckolls et al., 1972; Rabkin and Struening, 1976; Barrera, 1981; Dean and Lin, 1977; Dohrenwend and Dohrenwend, 1980). Obviously, we cannot say that the lack of a social network or close social support system would cause health or mental health problems, but there is certainly a diversified body of research that indicates that there is some consistent pattern of relationship between social networks, health, and mental health. Each of these reasons will be examined in Chapter 3.

DISENCHANTMENT WITH PROFESSIONALS

The community mental health center movement began in the early 1960s with the expectation that it would be a bold new step in the mental health system. It was envisioned as a system of easily accessible community- and family-based programs that would help keep people in the least restrictive and cheapest environment with their own family and friends (Joint Commission on Mental Illness and Health, 1961). It was also to serve as a center for advocating for causes and concerns relevant to the community and its residents. Furthermore, it was meant to prevent everything from teenage pregnancies and drug abuse to family stress and job burnout. Trying to be all things to all people subsequently caused it to lose its effectiveness in the eyes of many.

Perhaps the most obvious place where people have turned away from the professionals in recent years has been in politics. Presidents in recent elections were elected largely on the basis of saying that they would take government out of the hands of the professional bureaucrats and return power to the people. The "people," it seems, have now been given too much incorrect information. Expert economists rarely agree and often mislead people who trust their predictions with their careers and/or their life savings. Expert psychologists seem to reverse themselves totally each generation in their advice to parents raising children. Experts in sociology still see major revolutionary social movements every four or five years that nearly contradict each other, from Reich's *Greening of America* (1970) to Lasch's *Culture of Narcissism* (1979) to Yankelovich's *New Rules* (1981). Expert stockbrokers have been found to have investment records for their clients based on little more than random choice. Experts in education seem to be criticized constantly by parents who feel that teachers no longer know how to educate their youngsters or even how to maintain discipline in the classroom.

Perhaps the greatest disappointments have been the "experts" in mental health and social services. A Nader report (Chu and Trotter, 1974) entitled *The Madness Establishment* has documented how the experts in psychiatry and psychology, in particular, very adeptly coopted the community mental health movement when it was first begun in the 1960s. That movement was officially begun with President Kennedy's Joint Commission on Mental Illness and Health and its *Action for Mental Health* (1961), which very clearly and rather idealistically envisioned a new order as the result of a brave new step in the treatment of mental illness. It supported getting people out of hospitals and back into communities with their families and friends.

The Nader report indicated that schools of psychiatry were particularly threatened by this, in spite of the well-documented benefits to patients. Rather than help lead the way towards more humane and beneficial care by using the social networks and support systems of individuals, the experts in universities and in professional organizations managed to use their expertise, as well as their political pull, simply to maintain the status quo and undermine the new emphasis on community care. They used the federal funds earmarked for educating professionals in these new community-oriented approaches to continue teaching instead the long-term, one-to-one, psychoanalytically based treatments that had become and continue to be the most lucrative for those in private practice.

For the most part, it is unfair and inaccurate to impugn the morals or motivation of the experts. Politics, economics, psychology, sociology, and education are far from exact sciences, and the professionals in each of these fields tend to express whatever their data or sources of information indicate to them is true or realistic. However, these experts are dealing with the human equation, and few would be so bold as to claim that they have "the answer" and that it is irrefutable. Yet the lack of an answer for this increasingly sophisticated, educated, and anxious citizenry inevitably leads to disenchantment. They want the answer, not a variety of authoritatively expressed expert opinions. In a vacuum of reliable answers from experts, people have turned to each other, to their own social networks, for hope and help.

SELF-HELP: SUCCESS BREEDS SUCCESS

Another reason for the continued development of networking approaches is that networking is a form of self-help, and self-help movements are definitely continuing to grow (Gartner and Riessman, 1981). Most of the direct work is still done by the people concerned, but a social worker or psychologist may be there to help make the linkages and encourage the chain reactions. Also, networking is a common process in self-help groups, and the term is used frequently in relation to them. Borman (1982: 26), referred to "a recent review that we have undertaken of some major self-help networks that focus around particular afflictions or conditions (such as alcoholism, child abuse, heart surgery, and mental illness) indicates that distinguished professionals have often played important roles in initiating, advising, legitimizing, and guiding a group's development."

There are at least four different types of self-help groups. The first is for fund-raising, such as the March of Dimes. The second is for political activity, such as the National Organization for Women (NOW). The next is for social advocacy, or for changing public attitudes, such as the many gay rights groups and groups of parents of the retarded or of the institutionalized. Finally, there are the mutual aid groups that provide social, emotional, and even (indirectly) therapeutic help to one another as they support each other and discuss and work through common problems.

The growth of self-help has been tremendous. It is estimated by some that there are three-quarters of a million such groups, with a total membership of 15 million (Langton and Peterson, 1982). There are now self-help groups for all seventeen of the World Health Organizations disease categories. Various types of self-help groups are proliferating at a rapid pace in a wide range of areas. As families reconstitute themselves in ways and numbers that were unimaginable thirty years ago, we find self-help groups forming such as Stepfamilies, or Families Anonymous. Parents with special concerns join together in Parents Anonymous or Parents Without Partners.

Widows, who were so frequently ignored by professionals and subtly shunned by friends and relatives, now can choose from THEOS, the Widowed Persons Services, or Widows to Widows.

Self-help groups vary tremendously from those that want publicity and media attention, such as the National Gay Task Force, to those who seek to remain at least personally anonymous, such as Alcoholics Anonymous or Emotions Anonymous. Some run their meetings in a highly structured format based on strict ideological beliefs, such as Alcoholics Anonymous or Recovery, Incorporated, whereas others are deliberately unstructured in their meetings and organizations, such as THEOS. Some charge a fee that is quite high and use professional techniques and staff, such as Smokenders, whereas most charge minimal fees and use no professionals, such as AA.

By definition, self-help groups are run by and for people who share a concern or problem; this excludes professionals who do not personally share the problem. However, professionals have devised a great many ways of working with self-help groups so as not to undermine their autonomy and self-reliance. These collaborative models will be described in depth in the chapter on networking with self-help, but they include everything from simply making one available as a resource person or friend (Silverman, 1980), to organizing and running the initial sessions (Gartner and Riessman, 1981), or even networking a whole system of self-help groups by coordinating their efforts and making their existence known to the community (Maguire, 1983).

Success breeds success, and as self-help groups grow and the level of distrust diminishes between the groups and professionals, continued growth of the movement can be envisioned. Since the experts do not seem to have all the answers, people have learned to count on their own network of fellow sufferers, and on family and friends for advice, information, services, and material aid. In other words, they have learned to help themselves.

There may even be a valid argument for those who have claimed that the professionalization of education, child care, health, and welfare has actually been a major force in undermining the traditional networks of communities. If one can go to the experts in each of these areas, no network is needed. However, as indicated in the previous section, people have become increasingly disenchanted with the professionals.

Self-help is also no doubt a political euphemism for the abandonment of government responsibility for those in need. But abdicating responsibility for those who cannot help themselves, and then rather cynically and naively saying that somehow someone in the informal network will help, is indefensible.

The reality of how and why the self-help movement is growing may well be due to a combination of factors that include both a turning away from the powerful forces and experts in government and among the professional elites, and the fact that government is so inconsistent in its commitment to social welfare (Langton, 1982).

People have also gone into self-help movements and mutual aid groups to gain power over their own lives. The feeling of helplessness that drives many into seeking help in the first place is often not sufficiently relieved when a professional takes over. Help for many must begin with the person in need helping him- or herself. For years, the issues of anomie, alienation, and powerlessness have been favorites of psychologists and sociologists. They are now finding that these feelings can be resolved by taking hold or by taking direct action. The "best" type of help, as has so often been discovered in clinical research, is for the professional to empathize, support, and guide the group as its members find their own way.

Self-help is also developing as a means of networking because volunteerism, which is another form of self-help, is also getting increased attention. However, the old stereotype of the volunteer as being strictly a middle-aged, middle-class white female who works at home is rapidly diminishing.

Survey researcher Daniel Yankelovich (1981) believes that there has been a major, pronounced shift in the way people think and behave in the last twenty or thirty years. Much was said and written in the mid and late 1960s about the popular, activist, volunteer-oriented peace marchers and civil rights advocates, and about the spirit of love and peace that some social scientists described. This supposedly changed somewhat in the mid and late 1970s, when a shift toward oneself, or toward strictly narcissistic or egocentric activities, was noted. Perhaps many of those same peace marchers and civil rights advocates had become disenchanted, disappointed, or simply "burned out." In any case, much was written to the effect that individuals cared only about themselves and were basically unwilling to help others.

Yankelovich's (1981) survey indicates that there is a prevalent attitude that seems to say that people will work to help as long as it is for their own cause. The results indicate that there is a large untapped resource of people who are able and willing to help if it is a problem or cause they personally support. The pre-1960s willingness on the part of some to volunteer their time and effort because it was a duty to society, and not because the involvement helped their own self-interests, is rapidly disintegrating. With over half the mothers in the country now in the paid work force, time and energy have become scant resources for those who previously volunteered. Some traditional volunteers are still there, but their reasons for helping might be quite different. The problem itself, sometimes very narrowly defined, is now more likely to be the motivating factor.

The National Forum on Volunteerism (Allen et al., 1980) noted numerous factors that impact dramatically on volunteerism and involvement in the self-help network. Among them are changing attitudes, values, and lifestyles, as well as inflation, the energy crisis, the growth of litigation, and continued resistance from paid staff against the natural sector. In their report, volunteering was very broadly defined as "any relatively uncoerced work intended to help and done without primary or immediate thought of financial gain" (Allen et al., 1980). This includes not only direct service by individuals, but also involvement in social advocacy groups, self-help citizen action groups, boards and operations of public and private agencies, and activities in a wide range of informal networks and helping systems. The authors established several broad themes, as well as some important conclusions about volunteerism and networks.

Among these conclusions were that freely volunteering one's time and energy continues to thrive as an important element, and that people are pulling out of their cynicism and reestablishing a commitment to others—a trend noted in the Yankelovich data. Furthermore, future trends in networking will be affected by inflation, energy shortages, and resistance by paid professionals who fear that networking strategies, self-help, and volunteers will take over their paid positions. The report suggests that the volunteer community is a critical factor in society and, if properly organized, it could have a strong impact on society, provided it is not hampered by institutional barriers. Volunteering, particularly in a variety of natural helping networks, is seen as a means of citizens gaining power, and this power can and should be enhanced by developing coalitions with organized labor, government, and business. Finally, self-help network advocates and volunteer leaders must plan and prepare for the future, develop linkages, and educate the public about the importance of self-help networking and its affects on people in a free society. The report emphasized that there is a need to overcome the feelings of powerlessness that people have and to renew their belief that they can make a difference at all levels of helping and decision making. In fact, the report stated: "Only when citizens feel that they have and are free to exercise that power can the other concerns of the volunteer community be effectively addressed" (Allen et al., 1980: 4).

The capability and willingness of people to go out of their way to help others, without any immediate, direct, or guaranteed way of paying back or reciprocating no doubt varies, even from one decade to the next. Therefore, it would be difficult to predict accurately when or under what circumstances people will link together with others for self-help. For instance, it might be safe to assume that when resources are very limited and stress is high, such as during wars and major economic depressions, networking might be limited. Yet at least anecdotal evidence would indicate just the opposite.

People will heroically work together even to help relative strangers when conditions warrant it. Self-help networking strategies have recently been scrutinized and developed partially because of economic factors, a disenchantment with professionals, and the retreat of governmental institutions from involvement in social services, and in mental health and other health areas. The use of the term "networking" may well be short-lived, yet the process of linking people together for a purpose that involves chain reactions has long been a dominant interpersonal factor.

What has changed and necessitated a more focused and precise use of such self-help networking strategies will be described in a more detailed way in the later chapters of this book.

SOCIAL WORK AND SELF-HELP: WORKING TOGETHER

Professional social work involvement with self-help appears to some to be a contradiction in terms. How can it be "self-help" if a social worker is helping?

There is in fact no contradiction in this process. The social work profession has a long and proud history of actively encouraging people to use and develop their own resources, whether these include friends and relatives or merely their own personal capabilities. The process is still self-help as long as the primary responsibility is on the client and the intervention is focused on getting clients to use and develop what they already have in order to help themselves.

There are four specific instances when the need for social work intervention with self-help are most clearly indicated. The first is where the individual clearly has no personal or material resources or is extremely deficient. The second is where the resources are not readily perceived by the person or where they are dormant. The third is where the problem is sufficiently serious so that professional social work assistance in developing the resources becomes crucial to successfully working through the problem. Finally, social workers must encourage the self-help capabilities of a client when the nonpersonal resources needed are not as available to the client as they are to a professional social worker.

DEFICIENT PERSONAL RESOURCES

Social workers frequently work in situations where a client is either socially isolated, economically deprived, or personally incapable of meeting societal demands. Under such circumstances the worker needs to develop those resources for the client.

Social contacts can be developed through church groups, social organizations, residential facilities, and community organizations. Social workers can encourage a client to join organizations that will broaden his or her scope of contacts. Even minor problems become overwhelming when an individual has no one with whom he or she can share concerns or discuss the everyday joys and sorrows of life. People who are particularly susceptible to this social isolation are those who have moved frequently or recently, and those who have been affected by the death of a loved one on whom they were dependent. Widows and recently divorced people frequently need little more than guidance and suggestions concerning where they might go to meet others.

Economically deprived people have always been the mainstay of social work services. Those who need food and shelter look to the social work profession to help secure them. Social workers need to examine with the client any jobs available that may be appropriate, any items of their own that might be sold or returned, and ways in which they can manage their finances so as to keep them self-sufficient. Needless to say, there are some who have no financial resources or means of supporting themselves, such as the severely physically or mentally impaired, or single parents with young children.

Social workers have no doubt been guilty in the past of failing to examine all possible means of having individuals help themselves economically. Welfare should be a last resort, reserved only for those who have no other options available to them. The physically, mentally, or intellectually handicapped can work and in most instances desperately want the opportunity to be self-sufficient and independent. It is the social worker's responsibility to explore work training programs, sheltered workshops, and jobs that are not related to a person's handicap or disability. For instance, I know of blind telephone operators, retarded who work in factories, single parents who provide day care along with caring for their own children at home, and wheelchair-confined individuals who work in high-technology jobs using computer terminals at home.

DORMANT OR UNPERCEIVED RESOURCES

People often fail to examine their own self-help resources and capabilities sufficiently. Social workers can help clients to review personal contacts, work associates, and friends from a client's past systematically and thoroughly, as well as relatives and past or potential sources of material aid.

Initially, when clients come in to see a social worker, they often feel that they have already exhausted their own resources and see no apparent other resources available to them. However, I have found that by simply helping people to map their own social network, as described in the previous chapter, one can help them to realize that they do in fact have resources, A sensitive, supportive social work interviewer can probe and suggest that before a client gives up on his or her own resources, that these should be analyzed carefully. The social worker will therefore ask the client to examine his or her own social network in depth.

In the mapping exercise, clients define contacts in five spheres of influence:

(1) family;
(2) friends;
(3) work associates;
(4) neighbors; and
(5) professional helpers.

The worker needs to probe each of these areas carefully with a client by using the Personal Networking Assessment Instrument, which is presented in Chapter 4. In brief, what this instrument does is organize the data needed to analyze and define actual dormant and potential network resources. One works with the client to analyze each individual systematically and thoroughly in each of the five spheres mentioned. Individuals are analyzed in relation to:

(1) their willingness to help;
(2) their social and emotional capabilities;
(3) their material resources and contacts;
(4) the frequency of contact (daily, weekly, monthly, and so forth);
(5) the duration of the friendship (months, years, and so forth); and
(6) the intensity, direction, and degree of affection and comfort.

Resources for self-help are often available that have not been used for long periods of time but that can be revitalized by carefully planned interviews. These resources will not be utilized unless a professional social worker is available to point out their existence and guide clients in their efforts to help themselves.

SERIOUS OR LONG-TERM PROBLEMS

In many instances it is not fruitful and could ultimately even be harmful for individuals to rely solely on their own self-help resources. Specifically, these are cases where a client is seriously psychologically disturbed and in need of professional clinical social work care, or in very sensitive situations where the outcome of discussions or actions can have long-term, significant consequences.

Self-help efforts need to be directed and guided by a social worker who is knowledgeable in the traditional social work areas of expertise, as well as in natural resources and networks. Even with social work guidance, self-help efforts cannot be used alone in instances of severely dysfunctional psychiatric disorders or of physical abuse or violence toward a spouse, child, or anyone else, including self-inflicted harm. In those instances, the appropriate clinical social work treatment must be applied in conjunction with self-help efforts.

A depressed, unemployed, middle-aged former steel-worker would therefore in all likelihood need to be seen on an individual basis, as well as in family therapy. He might also be referred to a psychiatrist for medication and be involved with a professionally led treatment group. All of this would still not preclude networking efforts geared to developing his own self-help potential.

Clinical depression is frequently associated with lethargy, dependency, and sleep disorders. Clinical research has supported the notion that those who are actively involved and motivated during treatment do better than those who are not involved or motivated. By explicitly placing the responsibility for improvement on the client and those resources that he or she can identify, one is more likely to break the cycle of lethargy while minimizing the potential for depending on the worker.

Alcoholism and drug dependency are also disorders that require professional treatment. The social worker will undoubtedly work with the family and the individual in treatment, but the social network should also be involved in a therapeutic manner.

DEFICIENT NONPERSONAL RESOURCES

Social workers are sometimes referred to as linking agents, and often these linkages are made with other people and systems for material goods that are unavailable to most clients. Social workers have knowledge of and access to resources through personal contacts and intersystemic relations or connections for obtaining material aid such as money, food, shelter, jobs, and information. It is unfair, inappropriate, and naive to rely solely on clients' self-help potential to find a job on their own when they have already been looking industriously for six months. Similarly, a client cannot be self-reliant when he or she is already in debt, out of food, and on the verge of being evicted with three small children. Social work intervention to maximize self-help efforts is clearly indicated.

The social worker's resources, combined with the client's resources, turn into a formidable pair. The client, with support and help from the social worker, can eventually define his or her own idiosyncratic strengths and resources. The social worker will simultaneously be reviewing professional contacts and resources that need to be provided to complement and augment those defined by the client.

For instance, a teenage single mother who has dropped out of high school and begun abusing or neglecting her small child may not be aware of the existence of a special educational program in the area for just such women, or of the existence of a young parents' support group sponsored by a local social work agency. Such nonpersonal information resources are in fact rarely known by the public, who have no linkages with the professional social work community. Self-help alone would not be sufficient because the young woman would probably not know where to go for help or how to ask for it from her own circle of friends and associates. In fact, she may have been given misinformation or poor advice by friends and relatives, and without a social worker to help guide her in these important decisions, she may have done things that would negatively affect her and her child for many years to come.

Social workers can provide tangible resources such as money, food, and shelter, as well as intangible but nonpersonal resources such as information and job leads. None of these resources can be as efficiently or effectively developed by a client relying on his or her own resources alone.

REFERENCES

ALLEN, K. K., J. L. DUTTON, G. MANSEN, L. J. PETERSON, and W. D. RYDBERG (1980) The Shape of Things to Come, 1980-1990: A Report from the National Forum on Volunteerism. Washington, DC: The National Center for Citizen Involvement.
ANTONOVSKY, A. (1979) Health, Stress, and Coping. San Francisco: Jossey-Bass.
BARNES, J. A. (1972) Social Networks. Reading, MA: Addison-Wesley.
BARRERA, M. (1981) "Social support in the adjustment of pregnant adolescents: assessment issues," in B. Gottlieb (ed.) Social Networks and Social Support. Beverly Hills, CA: Sage.
BOISSEVAIN, J. and J. C. MITCHELL [Eds.] (1973) Network Analysis: Studies in Human Interaction. The Hague: Mouton.
BORMAN, L. (1982) "Leadership in self-help/mutual aid groups." Citizen Participation 3 (January/February).
CAPLAN, G. (1974) Support Systems and Community Mental Health. New York: Behavioral.
CHU, F. D. and S. TROTTER (1974) The Madness Establishment: Ralph Nader's Study Group Report on the National Institute of Mental Health. New York: Grossman.

DEAN, A. and N. LIN (1977) "The stress-buffering role of social support: problems and prospects for systematic investigation." Journal of Nervous and Mental Disease 165(6): 403-417.
DOHRENWEND, B. S. and B. P. DOHRENWEND [Eds.] (1980) Life Stress and Illness. New York: Neale Watson.
FISCHER, C., R. JACKSON, C. STUEVE, K. GERSON, and L. JONES (1977) Networks and Places. New York: Free Press.
GARFIELD, S. and A. BERGIN (1978) Handbook of Psychotherapy and Behavior Change: An Empirical Analysis (2nd ed.) New York: John Wiley.
GARTNER, F. and A. RIESSMAN (1981) Help: A Working Guide to Self-Help Groups. New York: New Viewpoint Books.
GOTTLIEB, B. (1981) "Social networks and social support in community mental health," in B. Gottlieb (ed.) Social Networks and Social Support. Beverly Hills, CA: Sage.
GROSS, M. (1978) The Psychological Society. New York: Random House.
HOLLAND, P. W. and S. LEINHARDT [Eds.] (1979) Perspectives on Social Network Research. New York: Academic Press.
Joint Commission on Mental Illness and Health (1961) Action for Mental Health: Final Report of the Joint Commission on Mental Illness and Health. New York: John Wiley.
KATZ, A. (1982) "Self-help and human services." Citizen Participation 3 (January/February).
LANGTON, S. (1982) "Self-help in perspective." Citizen Participation 3 (January/February).
——— and J. PETERSON (1982) "What is self-help?" Citizen Participation 3 (January/February).
LASCH, C. (1979) The Culture of Narcissism. New York: W. W. Norton.
LIEBERMAN, M. and L. BORMAN (1979) Self-Help Groups for Coping with Crisis. San Francisco: Jossey-Bass.
MAGUIRE, L. (1983) "Networking for self-help: an empirically based guideline," in F. Cox et al. (eds.) Tactics and Techniques of Community Practice (2nd ed.). Itasca, IL: F. E. Peacock.
——— (1981) "Networks and self-help groups," in M. Nobel (ed.) Prevention in Mental Health and Social Work. New York: Council on Social Work Education.
NUCKOLLS, K. B., J. CASSEL, and B. H. KAPLAN (1972) "Psychosocial assets, life crisis, and the prognosis of pregnancy," American Journal of Epidemiology 95: 431-441.
POLLARD, W. (1978) A Study of Black Self-Help. San Francisco: R & E Research.
President's Task Panel Reports (1978) Stock No. 040-000-00391-6, Vols. I-IV. Washington, DC: Government Printing Office.
RABKIN, J. and STRUENING (1976) "Life events, stress, and illness." Science 194 (December): 1013-1020.
REICH, C. (1970) The Greening of America. New York: Random House.
SILVERMAN, P. (1980) Mutual Help Groups: Organization and Development. Beverly Hills, CA: Sage.
WELLMAN, B. (1981) "Applying network analysis to the study of support," in B. Gottlieb (ed.) Social Networks and Social Support. Beverly Hills, CA: Sage.
YANKELOVICH, D. (1981) New Rules. New York: Random House.

Chapter 3

SOCIAL NETWORKS AND SOCIAL SUPPORT

PROBLEMS OF THE MENTAL HEALTH AND SOCIAL SERVICES SYSTEM

Since Eysenck (1952) first published his review of treatment outcome studies indicating that patients recover at approximately the same rates whether they are in treatment or not, the effectiveness of treatment in the mental health system has been debated. This problem has not as yet been positively resolved, and in fact, the literature indicates rather conclusively that at least the long-term psychodynamic approaches are very poorly supported in research (Garfield and Bergin, 1978). Yet 60 percent of the current practitioners in mental health still consider themselves to be psychodynamic. The public is becoming increasingly aware of this recently, and several scathing indictments by non-mental health professionals have recently attacked the "psychological society" of professionals not only for their poor treatment outcomes (Gross, 1978), but also for their professional organization's refusal to change and adopt new ways to utilize community supports (Chu and Trotter, 1974).

It is still true that there is a tremendous need for professionals to deal with the mental health, health, and social service needs of the populace. Serious social and emotional problems require advanced, specialized skills that can be achieved only through a high degree of professional training. In mental health, only a trained professional clinical social worker, psychologist, or psychiatrist who understands the etiology of severe emotional or psychiatric disorders is competent to treat patients. Within the medical field, only a doctor or nurse has the advanced knowledge of human anatomy to help patients with the type of treatment that will save lives, mend broken bones, or treat wounds. Similarly, in social services a knowledge of human service systems, organizations, and resources is required. To link people in need with the resources to grow rather than just survive, or to provide aftercare at home or in a sheltered environment for the physically, mentally, or psychologically incapacitated requires a professionally trained social worker. But there is considerable doubt that the limited professional resources that we have are being efficiently and effectively utilized.

In spite of precipitously rising health costs in recent years, the United States ranks poorly in the overall quality of care in industrialized Western nations, and it alone stands as the only modern Western country that has no organized child care system. Our public welfare system is generally denounced as inadequate, inept, insensitive, and bureaucratic. Poverty, hunger, and inadequate housing still abound in this country, and such problems appear to be increasingly exacerbated. The vast professional mental health system is also receiving tremendous criticism for its poor results. The cost of human services, as well as health and mental health programs in the current professional system, is becoming prohibitive. In spite of the fact that the health care system of this country is rapidly rising, politicians are rarely inclined to seriously challenge the medical health care industry. The less politically powerful social services lobby has seen human services cut while the cost of the welfare system has risen as payments to recipients have necessarily increased. The aged, poor, deinstitutionalized, and minorities no longer have access to many government-financed services and cannot afford such services from professionals in private practice or from the profit-making professional sector.

Within the formal mental health and social services systems, there have also been numerous attempts to examine how a client's or patient's social support system or network affect him or her in relation to the outcome of therapy (Maguire, 1979).

While therapists and mental health professionals have developed approaches that recognize and frequently involve the social support systems of clients—such as the psychosocial approach, applications of ego psychology, family therapy, and some forms of group therapy—there is relatively little recognition of the direct clinical utilization or manipulation of social supports and networks.

The first research attempts to evaluate treatment outcomes were in the early 1900s. Primarily, they looked at the effectiveness of the psychoanalytic approach, which is innately difficult to evaluate in terms of outcome due to its reliance on intrapsychic phenomenon; hence, research in the field was inconclusive. Various projective techniques such as the Thematic Apperception Test (TAT) or the Rorschach purported to assess the underlying psychopathology, yet the reliability of such measures has always been suspect (Strupp and Bergin, 1969), and the cost and difficulty of administering them have kept them from more widespread use.

Even when extensive research studies are published that review, summarize, and critique other research on mental health services, there is always extensive debate over the interpretation of results. For instance, in relation to Eysenck's (1952) original study, which has had a profound effect on mental health professionals even to this day, there was extensive debate and criticism of how he analyzed the results of the studies (Bergin and Lambert, 1978). Eysenck did not count the "slightly improved" as improved; eliminated the dropouts, which account for three-fifths of the cases among lower socioeconomic status clients; and eliminated nonneurotics. Bergin and Lambert (1978) took Eysenck's data, which contained the results of 24 articles using 8053 cases, and by using slightly different criteria for success in interpreting one of the studies at the Berlin Institute, found a 91 percent improvement rate, as opposed to the 39 percent that Eysenck reported. Since methodologically rigorous empirical evidence is rare and open to considerable interpretive leeway, the debates in the journals and elsewhere are emotional but generally nonproductive. These concerns have been considered extensively, and evaluation guidelines for treatment have been established (Waskow and Parloff, 1975).

In spite of these methodological issues, there are certain obvious variables relevant to networks that must be examined in order to assess the social support effects on treatment outcome. Since most of the research indicates that no social support variables singularly account for much of the variance in outcome results (Bergin and Lambert, 1978; Maguire, 1979), the interaction effects between and among variables must be examined. For instance, marital status, which can be used as a rough means of social support, is not significant alone in relation to how well one does in treatment, because marriage differentially impacts on males and females, and on different age groups. Socioeconomic status also has a significant impact in relation to both treatment outcome and social supports, so that when examining the interrelated effects of social supports and treatment outcome, research must assess not only outcome measures, marital status, or living arrangement, but also their interaction effects in relation to age, sex, and socioeconomic status.

In spite (or perhaps because) of these methodological issues and the resultant inconclusiveness of the effectiveness or lack of effectiveness of the formal counseling, social services, and mental health systems, many feel that those systems have been a disappointment. Even the advent of the community mental health center movement, which took a "bold new step" in recognizing the tremendous significance of family, neighbors, friends, and others as resources (Joint Commission on Mental Illness and Health, 1961), has seemingly lost some of its own support from those who share the same beliefs but feel that the formal service system has somehow failed (President's Task Panel Reports, 1978). The very basis of the formal helping system has been challenged. Professionals' lack of knowledge and insensitivity to networks, community support systems, extended family, work colleagues, and so forth has not only helped to undermine their credibility, but paved the way for the political and economic factors that have led to decreased support or funding of the formal system.

New approaches using networks of people to help themselves need to be developed, and this can only be done by combining the resources, strengths, and differing areas of expertise of both formal and informal helping systems. Before those strategies can be successfully implemented, however, the bases for those strategies must be better understood. The next section will examine some of the methods used to measure and analyze social networks.

SOCIAL NETWORK ANALYSIS: PURPOSE, PROCESS, AND STRUCTURE

Social network analysis is not a purely academic exercise. Its implications for practice are profound. The knowledge developed by anthropologists and sociologists such as J. A. Barnes, Elizabeth Bott, Barry Wellman, Claude Fischer, and J. Clyde Mitchell have provided invaluable detailed insights for networkers into the ways in which the natural networks of relatives, friends, neighbors, colleagues from work, and casual acquaintances relate to each other. Much of this information, and even its methods, can be used now to assess the capability of an individual's or family's network in order to encourage it when networking is appropriate.

By more clearly analyzing the structure, interactional patterns, and functions of intimate, socially supportive relationships, one can ultimately develop strategies that strengthen networks where they exist, develop them when they are needed, and leave them alone when they are working. The network concept itself is not of recent origin, but the interest in it by applied social scientists, particularly psychologists and sociologists, as well as social workers, psychiatrists, and nurses, has increased markedly in the past few years.

In this section of the chapter we will examine how the development of the methodology of social network analysis itself has helped in the rise of networking strategies. It has helped in three ways. First, through social network analytical methods, we are now able to establish more precisely the specific purposes and functions of different types of networks or network configurations. Second, social network analysis has helped us to understand the process of how people make connections. Third, it has given us a way to understand certain structural patterns of the organization of networking so that we can compare and contrast them. We will briefly explore examples of how social network analysis examines the purposes and functions of networks for widows, the processes involved in developing friendships, and the differences in the structure of networks for "normals" as opposed to those for psychiatric patients.

PURPOSE

In the Walker et al. (1977) study, which considered the purposes and functions of social support networks in coping with the bereavement of widows, the authors examined five different types of relationships between individual needs and specific characteristics of networks. They found that, first, networks help to maintain a social identity. A relatively unchanging and uncomplicated identity is maintained by a small, dense, culturally homogeneous, lowly dispersed network with strong ties. The practical implications of this finding for networkers are that such closely knit networks can be very supportive and helpful but are less likely to encourage change or provide help or resources in circumstances that are not familiar to the network members. For instance, such a network might be of little use if a member needed a good tax lawyer, information about a job in a specific industry, or even the advice and empathy of a friend who has just endured the initial shock of the death of a spouse. Under each of those circumstances, a larger, more heterogenous, and more widely dispersed network with looser ties is required.

Second, it was generally found that certain characteristics of networks are related to emotional support, and that the high "density and homogeneity of a network should increase the likelihood that network members are aware of and discuss the problems of members and agree concerning the best means for providing emotional support" (Walker et al., 1977: 36). Dense networks tend not only to have more frequent contact among its members, but that contact involves a greater degree of involvement, intimacy, and emotional attachment. Physical proximity is also a factor, in that social or emotional support is more likely to be given by someone who lives nearby, other factors being equal.

The third area, dealing with research or material purposes and services, indicates that, again, a more widely dispersed, larger network is more likely to supply a wider variety of supplies and resources, but that a high degree of density helps as well, since it supports communication within the network. The fourth function, and one that has been well studied by network researchers, involves information. When new knowledge or unusual information is required, a network is often used with at least some weak ties that bridge other networks. One or more weak ties to different types of networks increase the likelihood of encompassing different opinions, as well as new information, since close-knit personal networks are more likely to share the same opinions and information. This was an apparent factor in the *Gemeinschaft-Gesellschaft* distinctions that were studied by most sociologists some years ago. That research showed that the "locals" or the rural Gemeinschaft, were typified by the pre-Industrial Age village of cultural and ethnic homogeneity. The Gesellschaft, or cosmopolitans, were oriented toward the larger society and had interests and contacts outside the local community. They also had what networkers would call more numerous weak ties. The urban-dwelling Gesellschaft did have access to more diverse resources and information, though sometimes at the cost of the intimate social support provided by the tightly knit social network of close friends and relatives.

Finally, the fifth purpose that can be assessed in relation to network characteristic involves new social contacts. The difference between information and new social contacts is that the latter are sought for the purpose of developing strong ties or relationships, whereas information is more purely instrumental. New social contacts can be established at a place that is not linked to an individual's network of friends, such as a singles bar, but the reliability of the new social contacts is more likely to be increased if they are first screened through one's own personal or social network. One may need to remember this when attempting to broaden a social network. It is possible to use existing network members as bridges to new social contacts, thus helping with the transition as well as insuring that the new social contact will be a compatible network member.

PROCESS

Other social network analysts have provided equally useful findings for networkers. For instance, there is a "choice constraint" model (Fischer et al., 1977) that looks at the process of developing or maintaining networks. This theory proposes that one chooses his or her social relations and network members on the basis of certain limited alternatives and limited resources. Individual choices vary with their preferences as well as their options. It is a person's views, opportunities, and constraints rather than simply geographic mobility or population density that decides with whom he or she will relate. Social networks are seen as more a product of individual choice in selection rather than an "a priori" structure or simple mechanistic cause-effect relations for guiding the choice of friends. This choice constraint approach emphasizes that networks are formed on the basis of rewards, costs, and social context. These factors all change continuously, based on such considerations as life cycles, death, moving, economic changes, and interpersonal events. Relationships are maintained as long as the costs do not go too far and exceed the rewards. If the costs of maintaining the network and one's friendship increase (for example, one person moves) or the rewards decline (for example, one friend loses interest in a mutual hobby or sport), the bond or link is likely to become weaker and the friends will see each other less often. Such considerations are extremely important for a networker in making a linkage. Individuals develop new linkages to new friends and networks based on shifts in rewards and costs, always seeking to maximize rewards and minimize costs.

Laumann (1973) surveyed 185 white men between the ages of 21 and 64 in the Detroit area living with their primary families. He found that longer-lasting friendships were more intimate and that intimate friends were seen more often. On the other hand, many friends who were known longer were seen less. The reason for this is that many of the early supports of a friendship, such as school, jobs, physical proximity, and so forth, deteriorate or are displaced over the years. Therefore, the friendships that are maintained in the absence of such strong role supports are only the intimate ones, those that the individual values enough to work at maintaining. Those are the most important and significant ties for the networker. Older people are particularly subject to this network loss, since more of their close friends and relatives are likely to be displaced over the years as a simple function of age and longevity. The childhood friends, siblings, and former colleagues who constitute their most intimate system of support are more likely to be lost to them than the friends, relatives, or other natural support system members of other age groups.

Laumann also found that the extent of multiplexity (which he defined as the number of role relations, such as friends, relatives, co-workers, neighbors, fellow association members, and so on, involved in a link) is not associated with either how long friends knew each other or how intimate they were. Men who knew each other longer actually tended to share fewer roles. Of new pairs of friends (three years or less), 40 percent shared three or more roles, including friendship, while of old friends (13 years or more), only 29 percent shared three or more roles. In fact, the greater the multiplexity, the slightly less intimate the friendship

In terms of duration, kin and childhood network friends were known the longest, for obvious reasons. Work, neighborhood, and association friends were known the shortest period of time. Furthermore, men perceived that kin and childhood friends were the most intimate, and that friends they had found in the work or neighborhood setting were the least intimate. It seems that work and neighborhood friends can be distinguished as a class apart from kin and childhood friends. Work or neighborhood friendships were short term, ethnically dissimilar, and not very intimate, but involved frequent contact. Kin and childhood friendships tended to be comparatively more ongoing, intimate, and ethnically similar for most populations, but were acted on infrequently. In some respects, these two types of friendships within networks can be classified as those of "convenience" as opposed to "commitment."

Dispersion, or the number of sources where people develop friendships (for example, work, kinship, neighborhood), was lower than if it had been the result of mere chance. Men tended to draw their closest friends from a single source, with 26 percent drawing all three friends from one source. Also, the more dispersed a respondent's network, the less dense it was likely to be. In other words, the greater the number of sources that produce the friendships, the less likely it is that these friends will be friends of one another. Furthermore, there are two types of network sources that differ in their relative constraints. Laumann (1973) found that kinship and work networks were more constrained and produced high network density and low similarity, while more voluntary contacts such as childhood ties and associations allowed low network density and high social similarity.

STRUCTURE

The structural differences in the personal networks of "normals," psychotics, and neurotics have also been studied (Pattison et al., 1975). Normal people tend to have 20-30 people in their personal networks, while neurotics have smaller networks of 10-12, with neurotics themselves relating in a comparatively nonsystematic way to their networks. Psychotics had the fewest contacts (4-5), although their networks were quite dense, since they consisted almost entirely of family members. In Tolsdorf's (1976) research on the networks of two matched groups of hospitalized subjects, one of which was psychiatric, the other general medical, he found that the psychiatric patients were not reciprocal with their networks. They received some support, guidance, and help but provided little in return. The psychiatric patients' networks were composed primarily of family, and the members of their networks had to provide a greater diversity of support.

Overall, there does appear to be a qualitative and quantitative difference in the structural composition of the networks of those with psychological problems as opposed to those who are "normal." Whether structure and size have a direct or causal effect on the psychological well-being of individuals is not known. In short, we do not know whether the smaller and structurally different networks of more disturbed people are causative factors in the development of psychological problems, or whether, because of the preexistence of psychological problems, the structure never develops into a support network. The next section will examine the issue of social support systems as buffers against stress and the correlation between mental health and social support.

SOCIAL SUPPORT NETWORKS IN HEALTH AND MENTAL HEALTH

Many authors have defined and measured that elusive concept called "social support" (Caplan, 1974; Cobb, 1976; DiMatteo and Hays, 1981; House, 1980), but there is still little agreement as to precisely what it is. Social support is *not* treatment (or even guidance), although it may include some aspects of both. It is a feeling and attitude, as well as an act of concern and compassion. It is what friends, good neighbors, and relatives provide. When these kith and kin link together for the purpose of helping, they form a social support network.

Without this informal network, professionals in the mental health and social services systems would be pitifully incapable of dealing with the problems that people present. In fact, the professional systems' proportion of overall help and social support for individuals is minute in comparison to the vast resources of existing social support networks.

The literature generally differentiates between personal or social support systems and community support systems. Personal or social support systems consist of friends, family, neighbors, and colleagues who provide support, help, and a personal care or concern for identifiable individuals. Community support systems consist of the supports or services provided within a community or neighborhood for helping residents to meet their own social-emotional needs, as well as general welfare concerns. Community support systems therefore consist of the resources within any given community that can be potentially tapped by individuals in meeting their needs.

One can also differentiate between personal or social networks and, for lack of a better term, "general" networks or natural helping networks within communities. A personal or social network is established and analyzed on the basis of a central figure or ego. The networker defines and graphs the network on the basis of the number of people known directly or indirectly to an identified central figure, and his or her intensity or emotional attachment can then be examined as illustrated in Figure 1.2. The bond or basis for a general network, on the other hand, is not an individual but an idea, a political or religious belief, a shared problem, concern, or ability, or ownership of needed resources. The key to networks is the pattern of linking and the nature of the multiple connections and their chain reactions. The concept of social support, on the other hand, stresses directly the type of help or resource provided, not how those helpers or resources are linked together by the networker.

The significance of a social support becomes apparent when it is examined in terms of its protective or buffering effects on an individual's health or mental health. Sidney Cobb (1976: 300) reviewed the considerable research on social support and its moderating effects on life stress, concluding: "It appears that social support can protect people in crises from a wide variety of pathological states: from low birth weight to death, from arthritis through tuberculosis to depression, alcoholism and social breakdown syndrome." Furthermore, he cited numerous studies throughout the life cycle that support this claim, as well as the statement that social support also helps to reduce the amount of medication required, speed up the rate of recovery, and encourage people to comply with their medical needs.

The relationship between social supports and health or mental health problems is not, however, a direct causal one. If a person has a high degree of social support, this does not necessarily cause him or her to be physically or mentally healthy. Instead, social supports serve as a buffer, so that people with a social support network of friends and relatives are seemingly protected somewhat from the effects of stress. There is a complex interaction of effects among the factors of social support, health or mental health, and the type and degree of stress or problem being confronted.

The interaction of social supports and life stresses is not yet totally understood, but it is particularly significant in considering the elderly, women, the poor, minorities, and chronic aftercare or psychiatric patients, whose frequently smaller social support systems make them highly susceptible to the negative effects of stress. In one study by Nuckolls et al. (1972), the interaction effects of stress and social support were clearly evident. They used the Holmes and Rahe Schedule of Recent Experiences, a questionnaire measuring psychosocial assets, and medical records to assess differences among women in relation to problems in pregnancy. They found that neither the life-change score nor the psychosocial asset score was related significantly to complications. However, 91 percent of the women with high life-change scores but low social supports had at least one complication, compared to 31 percent of the women with equally high life-change scores but high assets. They surmised that women with high assets or social supports are less susceptible to a variety of "environmental insults," although they are cautious to point out that several diverse factors must be considered.

Another study (Gore, 1978) took a longitudinal approach to look at the effects of unemployment on men with varying levels of support. The men were visited by public health nurses at five regular intervals over a two-year period beginning six weeks before termination and ending two years after their plant closing. Social support was measured by an index of the individual's perception of spouse, relatives, and friends as supportive; frequency of activity involving the relationships; and number of social activities that were satisfying or that provided an opportunity to discuss their problems. Also measured were level of depression, degree of self-blame, illness symptoms, and level of serum cholesterol. They found that the socially unsupported, while unemployed, had higher elevations of cholesterol level, illness symptoms, and affective responses. Those with social supports had lower levels and fewer symptoms.

Another study (Lin et al., 1979) looked at stressful life events and social supports, concluding that stresses are positively related to symptoms, and that social supports are negatively related. They measured stress as well, on a scale relating to 24 psychiatric symptoms. In their study of Chinese Americans, they also assessed social support using a nine-item scale of individuals' involvement and interaction with friends, neighbors, cultural community activities, and other primary nonkin supports. They found that when social supports are low and stress is high, more psychiatric symptoms are in evidence, and they concluded that social supports act as mediators between stresses and illness.

Cassel (1976) drew a similar conclusion in his review of a variety of related studies. In fact, he pointed out that in Holmes's research on tuberculosis, it was found that the disease was far more prevalent in "marginal" people, those who were deprived of meaningful contact or who were without close friends or relatives. Cassel also noted a higher susceptibility to disease among ethnic group members who were minorities in their neighborhoods, as well as among those who had undergone frequent occupational transitions or residential moves, or who lived alone or were single or divorced.

Social support networks and their relationships to mental health are even more difficult to define clearly, but they are essential for networkers to understand. Mental health encompasses one's perception of the quality of one's life and functioning or role performance relative to one's capabilities. It may also involve the presence or absence of psychiatric or abnormal symptoms.

One way of assessing mental health is through social survey research, which seems to support the idea that those who have supportive networks and systems comprising a spouse, family, and friends perceive the quality of their lives as somewhat better than those who do not (Campbell et al., 1976). However, this is very much affected by such factors as marital status, sex, and age. In examining some of their data, Campbell et al. (1976: 435-436) concluded that: (1) married women and men without children are more positive about their life experiences than never-married people of comparable age; (2) this discrepancy is greater among older men than older women; (3) never-married women are more positive than men of comparable age; and (4) never-married people do not become more positive about their lives as they grow older. Thus, the social support provided by marriage has its costs for both sexes. However, the costs of being single or without one ongoing, intimate relationship are even greater. If the single status follows a divorce, the subsequent loss is more problematic for females than males, although never-married men seem to find life the least satisfying of any group, particularly as they become older.

Campbell et al. concluded that the greatest differences were not between males and females, young and old, or married and single, but rather were due to a combination of each of these as well as other social support factors. For instance, while there were some clear differences between the sexes on several key mental health-related issues, the "healthier" scores received by some categories of males can be accounted for by their superior financial positions. To paraphrase, money cannot buy social support networks, but the absence of sufficient money or the belief that one is barely surviving economically can lead one to exerting a disproportionate amount of time and energy merely in order to provide for the necessities of life. In fact, in summarizing who is most likely to have a small nonkin network, Fischer and Philip have stated that it was usually those with low education, low income, the old, the married, and females. These characteristics are frequently interconnected, and there are many interaction effects. However, Campbell et al. (1976) did find that 60 percent of the divorced or separated women felt frightened, versus 29 percent of the divorced or separated men. In all, 42 percent of them felt that life was hard, compared to only 25 percent of the men and, of most importance in relation to networking, a full 25 percent of the divorced or separated women worried about nervous breakdowns, as opposed to only 8 percent of the divorced or separated men.

Bernard (1972), who primarily summarized and described the research of others, argues very persuasively that marriage is essentially mentally healthy for men but not for women. She documents how married men fare extremly well on nearly every index of mental health, whereas married women do not. In fact, married women do much more poorly than single women in nearly every indicator. The population that scores rather consistently low on both social supports and various indicators of mental health is that of single men, who become disproportionately less "healthy" as they grow older.

In the classic study by Gurin et al. (1960), the authors found that marriage was a very significant social support factor and source of help during unhappy times. Maried people, both men and women, were found to turn to another person during unhappy times, whereas single people did not. A total of 47 percent of the married men and 37 percent of the married women turned to someone else (usually their spouses), whereas only 20 percent of the single men and 28 percent of the single women sought help from another during stressful times. Marriage is a seemingly unique situation, and some single people do not turn to others because others are not felt to be appropriate; that is, other "kith and kin" within a community or potential social network are not sought out, and thus some single individuals are left with essentially no social network support.

There has also been some significant research examining the way in which certain sociodemographic and social support factors affect the outcome of treatment within the formal mental health system. This is an area that needs increased attention, since the whole basis for networking rests on the contention that formal and informal helping systems must combine their resources in order to maximize their efficiency and effectiveness. If positive treatment outcomes within the formal mental health or social services system are increased by networking, or by working with existent networks of friends and family, then networking approaches must be used and developed. A first step in validating such approaches would be to examine whether the existence of social support networks of patients has any positive effect on the outcome of treatment in the formal systems.

This becomes complicated due to the fact that there are significant outcome effects relevant to age, sex, marital status, socioeconomic class, and previous treatment, regardless of networks. For instance, for treatment outcome and age, it appears that older clients have poorer or slower release rates from the hospitals and that married people improve more than single people in treatment, particularly those living alone (Ellsworth 1972; Linn, 1970; Smith and King, 1975). Neither sex nor race alone have been found to be significant factors in treatment outcome, once other factors have been controlled (Bergin and Lambert, 1978; Botwinick, 1973). Treatment factors such as previous service and length of time in treatment have also been found to have an impact on treatment outcome. Married clients with little or no history of prior hospitalization have lower recidivism rates and shorter hospital stays. For long-term patients, however, marital status does not seem to have any effect (Luborsky et al., 1971).

When using such starkly definitive outcome measures as suicide rates, social support factors, at least as crudely defined in terms of either being married or not, become significant. In this country the suicide rate for single men is almost twice as high as the rate for married men, yet the suicide rate for single women is less than one and one-half times the rate for married women (Bernard, 1972). Botwinick's (1973) study of race, sex, and age in relation to suicide rates is particularly striking, especially when graphed. One can see an almost perfect positive linear relationship for white single males. White males commit suicide at an accelerating rate as they get older. No other group follows that direct a pattern, nor at anywhere near as high a rate. At least for men, therefore, there seems to be some support for the positive effects of marriage as a social support.

In order to examine more precisely the effects of social support on treatment outcome, this author initiated some research in Ann Arbor at the Washtenaw County Community Mental Health Center (Maguire, 1979). The project was funded by the National Institute of Mental Health through the Michigan Department of Mental Health. The research was conducted as a part of the center's own management information system, so data were available not only on client demographic and background history (such as previous treatment episodes), but also on the type of treatment received, the amount of time in treatment, and the worker to whom they were assigned.

The dependent variable in this study was assessed using an instrument containing 25 general "problem areas" such as anxiety, depression, drug or alcohol abuse, sexual problems, and so forth, and five role areas. Of the 2745 subjects originally rated at intake on this instrument, 448 adult and children's cases completed the course of treatment and were rated when data collection ended. The rest were still open, referred later to other agencies, or dropped out. These results are similar to other research indicating that approximately two-thirds of the lower SES clients drop out before treatment would have formally terminated (a figure which, by itself, presents a strong argument for networking with existing supports as opposed to using the formal system). More than half of the 2745 cases were still being treated when these results were examined. All cases analyzed were rated for global functioning, which is a very general assessment of outcome that takes into consideration both objective and subjective measures of how a person generally functions or behaves.

The final outcome scores indicated a range of change in scores from one subject who improved a full four points (that is, went from a score of "1" to "5" from intake to closing) to the four subjects who ended two points "worse" than when they were rated at intake. A total of 37.4 percent of the adult clients (N = 206) made no change, 34.3 percent got slightly better or improved by one point, and 23.1 percent got much better or improved 2, 3 or 4 points by the time they finished treatment.

When we look at global change scores for adults only by sex in relation to marital status, which was used as one of the proxy variables for social support, we find that the single men did rather poorly in comparison to the single women or married men, although not at any statistically significant level. Only 51.7 percent of the single men improved, as opposed to 64.7 percent of the single females and 65.8 percent of the married males. Married women improve about as much as single women, but not as much as married men. In short, marriage seems fairly good for men but not quite as good for women.

Furthermore, it appears that previously married men (divorced, separated, or widowed) seem to improve more than previously married women, with combined "slight" and "much improved" scores for men of 69.3 percent, versus 47 percent for women. More than half of the previously married women either did not improve at all or became worse, as opposed to only 36.2 percent of the married females and 35.3 percent of the single females.

Another variable that may be considered as an aspect of one's social support system is one's living arrangement. Here the effects are really quite dramatic. For adults who live alone, the effects are potentially quite damaging for women, 28.6 percent of whom actually do worse or regress during treatment. Since the number of subjects is so small, the results should be considered cautiously. However, in comparison to men who live alone, women fare poorly. It also appears likely that females who live alone are the previously married—a group that has the worst improvement rate for women in relation to marital status. Finally, it appears from these results that it is not so much one's marital status per se that is important, but rather one's living arrangement or living within a social support network. Networkers will never have to be marital matchmakers, particularly for women, but they may at times need to encourage more supportive living arrangements.

The results of this research are certainly not dramatic, but it would appear that one's living arrangement, or living with one's own family, may positively affect treatment outcome. Furthermore, there is some support that previously married women who live alone are very much at risk in traditional treatment programs, and that married men tend to do relatively better. Clearly, more research needs to be performed in this area. Also more needs to be developed in relation to clinical or direct practice interventions, and to how professionals in the mental health and social services can engage social networks more actively in treatment.

REFERENCES

BERGIN, A. E. and M. J. LAMBERT (1978) "The evaluation of therapeutic outcomes," in S. Garfield and A. Bergin (eds.) Handbook of Psychotherapy and Behavior Change (2nd ed.). New York: John Wiley.
BERNARD, J. (1972) The Future of Marriage. New York: Bantam.
BOTWINICK, J. (1973) Aging and Behavior. New York: Springer.
CAMPBELL, A., D. E. CONVERSE, and W. L. RODGERS (1976) The Quality of American Life: SSA Edition. Ann Arbor, MI: Institute for Social Research.
CAPLAN, G. (1974) Support Systems and Community Mental Health. New York: Behavioral.
CASSEL, J. (1976) "The contribution of the social environment to host resistance." American Journal of Epidemiology 104(2).
CHU, F. D. and S. TROTTER (1974) The Madness Establishment: Ralph Nader's Study Group Report on the National Institute of Mental Health. New York: Grossman.
COBB, S. (1976) "Social support as a moderator of life stress." Psychosomatic Medicine 38: 300-314.
DiMATTEO, M. R. and R. HAYS (1981) "Social support and serious illness," in B. Gottlieb (ed.) Social Networks and Social Support. Beverly Hills, CA: Sage.
ELLSWORTH, R. B., H. R. DICKMAN, and K. J. MARONEY (1972) "Characteristics of productive and unproductive remit systems in VA psychiatric hospitals." Hospital and Community Psychiatry 23: 261-271.
EYSENCK, H. (1952) "The effects of psychotherapy: an evaluation." Journal of Consulting Psychology 16: 319-324.
FISCHER, C., R. JACKSON, C. STUEVE, K. GERSON, and L. JONES (1977) Networks and Places. New York: Free Press.
GARFIELD, S. and A. BERGIN (1978) Handbook of Psychotherapy and Behavior Change: An Empirical Analysis (2nd ed.). New York: John Wiley
GORE, W. (1978) "The effect of social support in moderating the health consequences of unemployment." Journal of Health and Social Behavior 17: 157-165.
GROSS, M. (1978) The Psychological Society. New York: Random House.
GURIN, G., J. VEROFF, and S. FELD (1960) Americans View Their Mental Health. New York: Basic Books.
HOUSE, J. S. (1980) Work, Stress and Social Support. Reading, MA: Addison-Wesley.
Joint Commission on Mental Illness and Health (1961) Action for Mental Health: Final Report of the Joint Commission on Mental Illness and Health. New York: John Wiley.
LAUMANN, E. O. (1973) Bonds of Pluralism: The Form and Substance of Urban Social Networks. New York: John Wiley.
LIN, N., W. M. ENSEL, R. S. SIMEONE, and W. KUO (1979) "Social support, stressful life events, and illness: a model and an empirical test." Journal of Health and Social Behavior 20: 108-119.
LINN, L. (1970) "State hospital environment and rates of patient discharge." Archives of General Psychiatry 23: 346-351.

LUBORSKY, L., M. CHANDLER, A. AUERBACH, J. COHEN, and H. BACHRACH (1971) "Factors influencing the outcome of psychotherapy: a review of quantitative research." Psychological Bulletin 75: 145-185.

MAGUIRE, L. (1979) "Factors in successful treatment outcome in community mental health." Ph.D. dissertation, University of Michigan, Ann Arbor.

NUCKOLLS, K. B., J. CASSEL, and B. H. KAPLAN (1972) "Psychosocial assets, life crisis and the prognosis of pregnancy." American Journal of Epidemiology 95: 431-441.

PATTISON, E. M., D. FRANCISCO, P. WOOD, H. FRAZIER, and J. CROWDER (1975) "A psychosocial kinship model for family therapy." American Journal of Psychiatry 132: 1246-1251.

President's Task Panel Reports (1978) Stock No. 040-000-00391-6. Washington, DC: Government Printing Office.

SMITH, C. G. and J. A. KING (1975) Mental Hospitals. Lexington, MA: Lexington Books.

STRUPP, J. and A. BERGIN (1969) "Some empirical and conceptual bases for coordinating research in psychotherapy." International Journal of Psychiatry 7: 81-90.

TOLSDORF, C. C. (1976) "Social networks, support and coping: an exploratory study." Family Process 15: 407-417.

WALKER, K. N., A. MacBRIDE, and M.H.S. VACHON (1977) "Social support networks and the crisis of bereavement." Social Science and Medicine 2: 35-41.

WASKOW, I. and M. B. PARLOFF [Eds.] (1975) Psychotherapy Change Measures. Rockville, MD: National Institute of Mental Health.

Part II

NETWORKING: THE INTERVENTIONS

Chapter 4

NETWORKING WITH INDIVIDUALS

Kith and kin are the undisputed primary source of help for individuals. This is true whether we are talking about social support, advice, or the provision of material resources such as money, jobs, or housing. In this century we have seen profound technological advances, but some would argue that we have also seen a usurpation of the traditional role of kith and kin by professionals in a wide variety of areas. Rehabilitation counselors now help people to adjust and grow after serious medical problems when they return home. Vocational guidance experts now help people to learn marketable skills and find jobs. Specialized teachers provide the time and expertise needed to help individual children overcome learning difficulties in school. Social workers work with individuals, families, and groups in a wide variety of arenas related to social welfare, jobs, housing, health and mental health, counseling, and rehabilitation. All of these roles would have been performed by friends and relatives some years ago but are now performed primarily by professionals.

The present problem in the provision of such services is not that professionals do them. On the contrary, the professionalization of such services has been a tremendous aid in providing care in a far more efficient, effective, and equitable manner. The problem lies in not adequately involving the social network of kith and kin in the process. The professionalization of many services previously provided by family and friends is a help only if it makes the process work better or more to the advantage of the individual being helped. Presumably, professionals have the knowledge base and technical expertise needed to vastly improve the level of help, but they frequently lack the time to follow up in depth or to develop the personal contacts that are often required to individualize their services.

Caplan (1974) makes the point that people have a variety of specific needs, such as for love, intimacy, and affection, as well as for the satisfaction of feelings of nurturance and dependency, and for help with tasks. Most people cope and feel good about themselves as long as they maintain and develop connections with people through marriage, parenthood, and close friendships with neighbors, work colleagues, and friends from one's church, school, community, or cultural organization. These needs are also met through relationships with professionals such as doctors, lawyers, social workers, teachers, clergymen, and community leaders or other influential people. In the aggregate, all of these relationships form a social support system that protects the individual against disease. The factor that all of these relationships have in common is that the central person is treated as a unique individual. The person helped, the center of this network or aggregate of networks that form the support system, is cared for in a personalized way. This support system, uniquely provided to a person who has developed relationships with these other people, must be enduring or ongoing. A social network connotes a type of organization based around an individual that provides the love, affection, aid, and protection that the person needs.

When developing a network strategy for an individual, one needs to recognize that one is not merely providing services for a client—instead, one is helping a unique individual who is cared for by a social network of family and friends. Unfortunately, there is a rather widespread feeling that what professionalization may have gained in some areas was at the cost of the sensitivity and concern that these individualized social networks provided. Both the social network analytical technology, as well as the planned use of the individualized social network, must be used to develop the best strategy for individuals who are genuinely cared for by the network.

A social network implies a particular method of analyzing a given support system, as well as an implication that the system is linked together with multiple ties. The advantage in analyzing an individual's support system using a social network approach is that the networker can get a more precise understanding of those personalized relationships which, in the aggregate, form the support system. This is important because each of those individual ties or links in the network is different from every other one. Some will help, and some may be harmful. It is not enough to categorize relationships with family and friends and other caregivers. You need to know more about the content, process, and development of the dyadic relationships within the network that forms the social support system for a particular individual.

APPLYING SOCIAL NETWORK ANALYSES

A problem has developed in recent years related to using social network analyses to study social support systems for individuals (Wellman, 1981). Previously, we were limited to epidemiological studies that examined demographics and other variables in relation to certain symptoms, problems, or diseases. That research was useful, but little of it could be applied to practice. The ground-breaking work of Faris and Dunham (1939) and the later work of Srole et al. (1975) told us a great deal about "populations at risk" and gave us descriptions of precisely which groups of people were most likely to have specific health or mental health problems. Later work made us more aware of the importance of the supportive ties that provide individuals with specific feedback and that can help in a variety of ways under stressful situations (Dean and Lin, 1977). Nevertheless, it is not sufficient to define social support simply in terms of the number of types of social ties. Much of the research has ignored the situational and structural factors, as well as the process or nature of the relationships involved in those ties. It is not enough to know how many people an individual knows, or even whether the tie is based on kin or friendship links (Gottlieb, 1981). In fact, a problem exists because researchers have begun using social network analyses to define social support systems in a rather simplistic way, sometimes naively assuming that all ties are positive and all networks are social support systems (Wellman, 1981). It appears that our technical expertise in such methods as social network analyses is once again surpassing our limited capability for operationally defining the complexities of human interactions and relationships.

We cannot take the same technology related to social network analysis that anthropologists use and apply it unchanged to support systems that can be used for individuals in need. Anthropologists generally recognize the necessity to focus clearly on and delineate precisely what they are studying in a network. For instance, social network analyses have been used to study the ways that people found jobs within a very small network of friends, or how certain individuals found an abortionist, or why certain people from one African village moved to a city. In research, it is necessary to define the focus clearly, to define operationally in measurable terms the dependent and independent variables, and to control for any intervening variables and potential contaminants. The same must be done when analyzing the social network of an individual in order ultimately to help them, but additional subtle factors must be known as well.

Networkers also need to know how certain people feel about one another. Such terms are rightfully abhorred by researchers for their lack of precision, but when dealing with human relationships and interactions, which form the essence of networks, one cannot rely on frequently forced, and therefore somewhat inaccurate, data and compounded statistical errors to make judgments. Relationships change, and the types of analyses that may serve an anthropologist to examine patterns of communication and influence at a single, static time and place are not sufficient. Networking efforts will be most efficient and effective when the networker uses the technical capacity of certain social network analytic approaches to establish a baseline for intervention, but also uses human judgment or clinical experience to develop a strategy that will work on an ongoing basis in a fluid system. In other words, one needs to establish certain network-related factors first to establish a clear baseline of knowledge, and then to examine the complexities and nuances involved in those changing network patterns before he or she can develop a workable network interaction for an individual over an extended period of time. Since networking involves chain reactions and the latter are difficult to predict and control, it is important to follow the process as it develops and to encourage certain linkages while discouraging others.

This chapter will examine two different types of networking with individuals. These include networks that provide resources, jobs, personal services, and general help for people, and those that provide social support, guidance, and even treatment in relation to a concern, problem, or emotional disorder. While the names for these networking strategies may vary, they will be referred to here as individual networking for resources and jobs, and individual networking for interpersonal problems.

INDIVIDUAL NETWORKING FOR JOBS AND RESOURCES

Jobs. The successful career of many individuals is based on their ability to network early in their careers. Within the university system, as with nearly all others, success is a rather relative and subjective term, but minimally it involves a professorship at a good university.

In order to achieve success in a university system, one needs an entree into the various departments. In a more perfect world, the sole criterion would be ability. Fortunately, it is still the most important factor, but in a profession where so many are "able" yet few are chosen, ability is not enough. Networking is also needed.

The individual who knows several faculty at a particular university where he or she wants to teach stands a better chance of getting a position that could lead to success than an individual with no such linkages. Furthermore, the contact person's centrality or authority within the department is significant. If that contact person or friend is the dean or the most influential faculty member within the school or department, the likelihood of getting the position will be maximized.

As an example, a friend of mine who left one university because he was denied tenure was able to get an equally good or better position at a comparable university because of networking. I had worked closely with one of the key faculty at the second university and wrote a long reference letter, followed up by a phone call. It was probably the phone call, which in this instance was far more individualized and personal, that helped the most. My friend, whom we shall call Bill, did not know anyone at the new university but was already considered a more likely candidate than several others because he had the qualifications. It was this individual networking, however—where my friend Bill contacted me and I contacted Professor Jones, a key figure at the other university, who then contacted her dean and two or three other central faculty—that ultimately tipped the scale in his favor. This network is diagrammed in Figure 4.1.

In this diagram, Bill was in need of a job. He contacted me, and I contacted Professor Jones. I knew her to be an influential faculty member at the university where Bill was looking for a position. She in turn contacted her dean, who spoke with Professor A, who chaired the faculty search committee. Professor Jones also contacted Professor A, as well as Professors B and C, who were other key faculty members. The Dean and Professors A, B, and C spread the word to other faculty (Professors D-L) whose support was useful in Bill's acquiring the job. Individual networking alone could not (and should not) have gotten Bill the job, but where merit or ability is deemed to be equal and many applicants apply for a single position, the personal individualized process of multiple linkages and chain reactions on behalf of an applicant can frequently make the difference.

A great deal of attention in the popular press has been given recently to networking for jobs, particularly by feminists. Women feel at a disadvantage in finding good jobs because the "old boy network," which is not only highly effective but elusive as well, excludes them. Men have historically and traditionally been more accustomed to calling or otherwise contacting friends, neighbors, colleagues from work, or relatives when they need concrete or "non-emotional" resources. Feminists assert that women are only recently discovering the fact that good jobs are frequently acquired through good contacts. This is true whether one is referring to the job of chief executive of a multinational corporation, the presidency of a major university, a secretary in a steno pool, or a laborer at the steel mills. While in relation to finding jobs the old adage that "it is not what one knows but who one knows" is still abhorrent to some, there is undeniably some truth to it.

Many other examples of effective individual networking exist within the upper ranks of the military and in the Pentagon. This bastion of

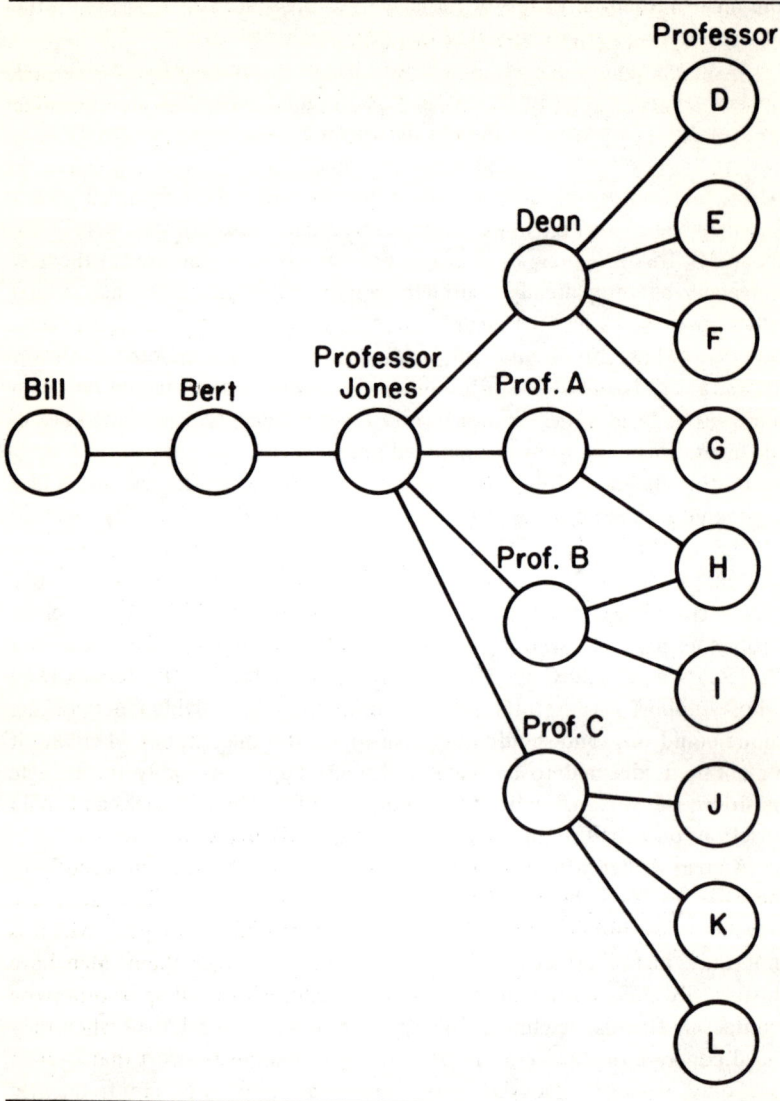

Figure 4.1: Networking for a Job: Faculty Position Example

power, which is even more dominated by males than the decidedly male-dominated business or corporate sector of America, is centered on the military academies of West Point, Annapolis, and the Air Force Academy. Upward mobility in the military is virtually confined to graduates of these academies, and certain graduating classes, such as West Point's class of 1915, which included both Dwight D. Eisenhower and Omar

Bradley, have seemingly established more densely knit and thus more supportive and helpful networks than others.

Women are quickly learning and even improving upon the male resources and job networks that exclude them. Through the National Organizationa of Women (NOW), the YWCA, and even the Chamber of Commerce in some cities, women are organizing feminist job networks throughout the country. Many have gone through difficult growing pains in which they have been criticized for the same types of exclusiveness that the old boy network displayed. For instance, the feminist job networks in some locales could not meet the needs of both the women who had been housewives and mothers for twenty years and were now returning to the work force with no marketable skills, as well as the twenty-five-year-old single females with MBAs and marketable skills but no entry into the male-dominated business network. This problem is being worked out in the same way that those of the feminist consciousness-raising groups of the 1970s were—by developing different chapters geared to different needs and interests.

Finally, another gender-related historical difference has been indicated in relation to team sports. In the past, men have had the nearly exclusive advantage of being socialized and acculturated into networking by being involved in team sports. While football remains almost wholly male, baseball, soccer, volleyball, and most other team sports are now beginning to involve females at a much earlier age and in greater numbers. The camaraderie, sharing, and intense mutual support and cooperation that is encouraged and developed among team members is an excellent basis for individual networking. There is a gradual realization among even young athletes that they can only succeed by helping and being helped by others.

Individual excellence on a team is beneficial to all, but there is nothing worse than a "hog" in basketball (that is, one who shoots too much and does not pass the ball to teammates), a "showboat" in football (that is, one who risks long passes or runs to get personal glory), or a "grandstander" in baseball (that is, a batter who will go for the riskier home run or long hit when the team has runners on base who need to be advanced home slowly, by "safe" ground balls or bunts). Team sports implicitly and explicitly require personal sacrifice for others and cooperation among players. By helping a teammate, players help themselves, since they are a part of the same unit or system. The same is true in networking. One only does well if one's teammates do well. If colleagues and friends in the same profession succeed, a newcomer can too, assuming that one's abilities are comparable, by networking.

Resources. Individuals rely on their social networks of family, friends, and neighborhood or work colleagues for a variety of practical resources and services. The resources may range from borrowing a cup of sugar to borrowing thousands of dollars, and the services may vary from asking a neighbor to sign a petition to asking a relative for consolation after the death of a spouse.

There are certain implicit rules and regulations governing the provision of resources and services from network members. Issues such as the longevity of a relationship, its number and types of ties (multiplexity), its origin (kin, neighborhood, work or professional, and so forth), the geographic distance involved, and the frequency of previous contacts all enter into the process (Fischer et al., 1977; Campbell et al., 1976; Craven and Wellman, 1973; Gurin et al., 1960; Kulka et al., 1979). The characteristics of the potential networkers are also significant since, for instance, the elderly are far less likely to network than other age groups, and women are far more likely to go to female kin than to anyone else for help with personal problems.

Individual networking for resources therefore depends on who is doing the networking and their purpose. In general, personal and emotional support and guidance is best provided by either long-standing, intimate friendship or kin networks. Material resources and less readily available or more technical resources or services must be provided by more diverse, less intimate, second-order networks, that is, network members known wholly or primarily through another or even a series of other contacts.

A woman with an unwanted pregnancy may turn first to her closest childhood friend for advice or emotional support. Another choice would be a friend, not necessarily as close, who has had an abortion. In either instance, she is ultimately likely to try to find a resource person to perform the abortion. This individual networking process usually involves a series of connections beginning with a discussion with a close personal friend, who talks to another person who has had an abortion, who then talks to a person who will perform the abortion (Lee, 1969).

The term "primary network" is sometimes used to refer to a network of people directly known by the ego or central figure, while a second-order network is composed of those more specialized caregivers known by the central figure only through others.

Typically, the type of individual networking for resources needed for social/emotional help would be composed of family and friends and would be quite dense, since the members would generally know each other. It could be diagrammed as in Figure 4.2.

On the other hand, if a woman needed to borrow resources such as a rotor tiller to dig up her yard for a vegetable garden, the relevant network would be quite different. If she knew that her brother and a friend of hers both knew the same neighbor who owned a rotor tiller, the network would look like that in Figure 4.3.

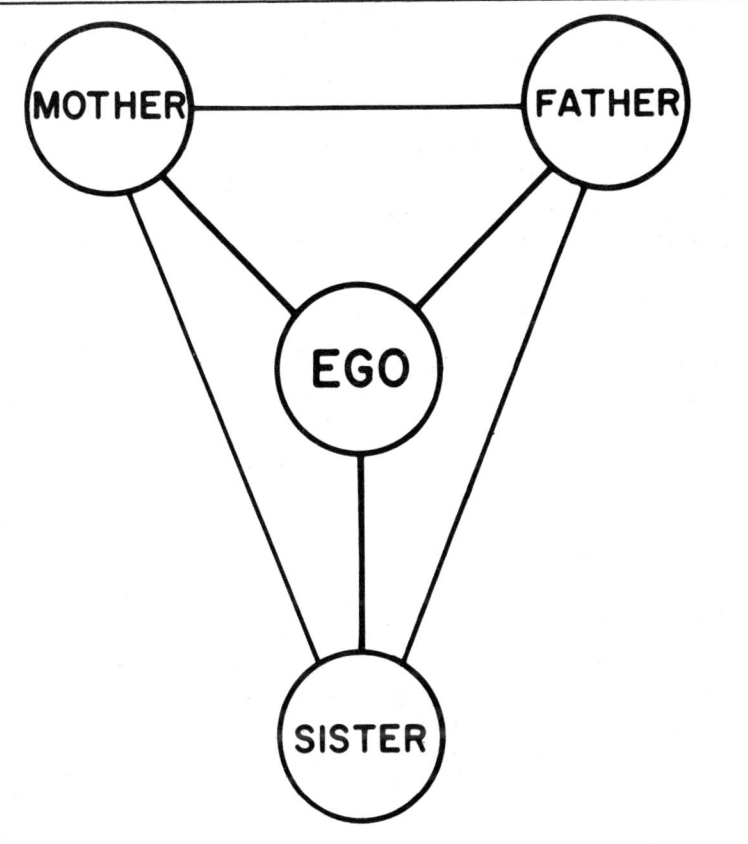

Figure 4.2

The figure alone only tells us that both the brother and the friend, who are members of the ego's social network, know a neighbor who owns the desired rotor tiller. That neighbor is a second-order network member who does not even know the ego. To network for that rotor tiller, the ego needs to first consider five network factors: size, basis of relationship, capabilities, resources, and level of willingness.

The *size* of the personal network is simply a count of those people whom the ego or central figure identifies as "possibly willing to help." It is established by asking the ego or central figure to identify potential network members on the *basis of relationships* in each of five spheres or areas of influence. These spheres are family or relatives, friends, neighbors, work colleagues, and other helpers. Networkers need to probe sensitively with the central figure the number of family members and relatives who

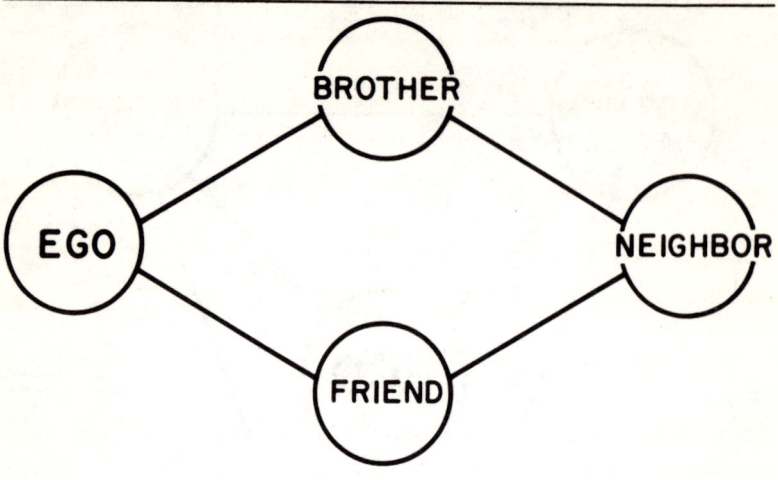

Figure 4.3

are possibly willing to help, the number of friends who are possibly willing to help, the neighbors, and so forth. The *capabilities* of the network members include their ability to provide resources and their access to resources. The *resources* themselves differ in that resources are more tangible than capabilities and can include money, housing or an extra room, a car, or such useful resources as personal contacts, access to jobs or information, or access to other professional or natural helping networks. The *level of willingness* to help is made explicit in the initial question to the central figure of the personal network. However, once the organizer and the central figure begin linking specific names to specific capabilities and resources, the question invariably arises as to whether others will actually be willing to use those capabilities or resources to help.

Men and women will no doubt continue to do individual resource networking and individual job networking in the same ways they have for years. With proper planning and a clear notion of what it is they are trying to accomplish, the networking process can yield far more resources or even job possibilities. This individual networking, therefore, requires the development of as many strategically placed connections as possible and includes joining and being actively involved in:

(1) *professional organizations,* such as the American Bar Association, the American Medical Association, the National Association of

Social Workers, the American Association of University Professors, the National Education Association, and others.
(2) *community organizations,* such as city- or suburban-sponsored civic activities, volunteer involvement in the PTA, Boy or Girl Scouts, the YMCA or YWCA, church groups, and/or local sports teams for one's children or for adults.
(3) *social-political organizations,* such as the National Organization of Women, the American Association of Retired Persons, and the Audubon Society.
(4) *ethnic-racial associations,* such as the NAACP, the Hibernians, or the local Italian-American or Polish-American associations that exist in every large city, especially in the northeast industrial cities.

Whether one is networking for the purpose of gaining resources for one's business, family, or self (such as a job), individual resource networking requires visibility and involvement in professional, community, and voluntary organizations of all sorts. It involves multiple connections and chain reactions.

Involvement in such activities must meet other needs of individuals, such as a desire to help their neighborhood school or improve their community's quality of life. Those immediate needs often take precedence over the acquisition of resources or a job, but it is likely that the plumber, lawyer, or secretary who is also the head of a Scout troop, treasurer of the PTA, or leader of the civic association is likely to be considered first by people who come into contact with them. For instance, a free-lance bookkeeper in my neighborhood audits the books and keeps many of the records for a half-dozen local community groups as a voluntary activity. She chooses to work part-time and only at home—two requirements that would automatically exclude her from the regular job market—yet this woman is continuously offered well-paying jobs from local businessmen and women to keep their books. Furthermore, when community groups need resources, they go to her because of her ability to network. Another neighbor, who is a lawyer, is actively involved in the school board and also happens to be hired by virtually all of the neighborhood to handle wills, house-buying and -selling, and the bigger, business-related litigation that frequently develops. A semi-retired carpenter who spent years volunteering his talent for numerous civic projects is now well paid by local people who know and respect him, and hire him to do everything from building bookcases to room additions. None of these people volunteer in these civic and community responsibilities to further their own incomes, or solely to get resources or a job, but it is no doubt an excellent way to maintain connections.

PERSONAL NETWORKING—
INDIVIDUAL NETWORKING IN TREATMENT

In order to most efficiently and effectively organize an individual's personal network for the purpose of aiding treatment, networkers need to identify potential networks, analyze them and their resources, and then link the person and the network into a more dense, caring, and knowledgeable support system. This can be accomplished through personal networking (Maguire, 1980).

Personal networking includes three phases: identification, analysis, and linking. However, before the intervention can begin, this understanding of the networking idea must be fully discussed and any reservations analyzed. People tend to be reluctant to engage their family and friends in this sort of individual networking process for the purpose of resolving social-emotional problems or concerns. This reluctance is based on many diverse factors.

First, they may be embarrassed about having a particular problem. For instance, if an individual is depressed over the loss of a job or a significant friend or relative, the depression itself and its concomitant disorders of sleeplessness, eating problems, crying, lethargy, or other symptoms may make the individual reluctant to have others see him or her at this time. Just the fact of being depressed is an embarrassment for some, particularly Americans, who are culturally discouraged from expressing such feelings.

The second reservation is based on a reluctance to ask for help. People are expected to work out their own problems without assistance from others, and a certain degree of reciprocity is at least implied in most interactional exchanges. To ask for help indicates for some the acceptance of a contract or agreement that they will return the favor in some way at some future time. Thus one becomes obligated by seeking help from the network. These concerns are all real and need to be discussed before any individual networking for treatment can be considered. Embarrassment can sometimes be addressed by discussing it and helping the individual to put it into perspective. For instance, if the central figure feels that his or her family will like him less or that their opinion of him or her will be lowered because of the depression, the networker needs to get the central figure to discuss the basis for this feeling. Has this happened before where people do in fact lower their opinions because one seeks help? Why would people do this? Who is most likely to feel this way? Openly analyzing and discussing the potential for embarrassment frequently leads one to recognize that the basis for the embarrassment, which is the presumed lowering of one's esteem within the network, does not necessarily happen, and that the problem is internally rather than externally based.

The reluctance to seek help is also a natural response and needs to be recognized as such. However, networking is not an admission of failure. Discussing times when the central figure has helped others in the past, and how they might in the future, can also be of value. However, the "tit for tat" notion is not to be encouraged. Focusing on reciprocity may be both ill timed and overwhelming for the central figure at the time, and it is a concept that is likely to be (inappropriately) literally defined due to the stress. In other words, people may feel that they will have to repay their network helpers "in kind" and at the same level or degree, when in fact the continuance of a friendship may be all the friend or relative really wants in return.

The particular types of problems for which personal networks are most appropriate are those that deal with interpersonal and intersystemic problems. This is not treatment per se but rather an auxiliary to it. It can be and usually is used in conjunction with other traditional forms of helping or treatment.

Personal networking both implicitly and explicitly recognizes the primary importance of one's existing or potential social network as a change agent or means of change. There is a curative or therapeutic message given to central figures when their friends and relatives can be rallied around them to join their efforts in effecting change. While the actual problem-solving itself should not be underestimated, the simple fact of networking may be sufficiently therapeutic or helpful in many instances to negate the need for any major work on the part of network members. To paraphrase Robert Vinter, networking is the means, not simply the medium of help.

Identification. The first phase involves identifying the potential for networking As discussed in the previous section of this chapter, the size, basis of the relationship, capabilities, resources, and level of willingness of the network members may all vary immensely. Each of these areas must be examined in the identification phase.

Initially, most people, including those with highly developed and supportive networks, may be unwilling or unable to supply many names. For this reason, a preface or introduction to personal networking is required. This introduction should include something to this effect:

> We have gotten together to try to work out your problem. (Briefly and empathically describe the problem, as stated by the central figure.) One way of doing this is by getting help from other people who care about you. It's not always easy to know who these people are, nor is it easy to ask them to become involved, but what I'd like

to do with you is to figure out what relatives, friends, neighbors, or people you may know from work might be able to come up with suggestions, advice, or other kinds of help.

The organizer then gives examples of the type of help which may be needed, but these must be conservatively stated in describing the level of help being sought.

The purpose of this identification phase is partially to gather information from which to develop a network analysis that will clearly define the network. However, it is also a necessary stage in establishing a basis and a relationship for further networking. Many people are reluctant to ask friends or relatives for help, so this initial or beginning phase of the personal networking process must be handled in a manner that is sensitive to the central figure's desire to avoid being a "burden" or "problem" to those who care about him or her. Many specific factors relevant to the personal network must be identified, but the identification must be done in a way that is conducive to developing a bond of trust between the organizer and the central figure, as well as among the organizer, the central figure, and the personal network itself.

Let us review the five factors to consider in the earliest stages of individual networking. These include the *size* of the personal network, or the number of possible connections. It is established by asking the central figure to identify potential network members on the *basis of relationships* in each of five spheres or areas of influence. These spheres are family or relatives, friends, neighbors, work colleagues, and other helpers. The organizer needs to discover with the central figure the number of family members and relatives, friends, neighbors, and so forth who are possibly willing to help. The *capabilities* of the network members include primarily their talent or acumen in being empathic or in showing care or concern, and in listening to a friend or relative and showing this genuine concern, as well as affection. The *resources* of the personal network member in this instance include personal contacts, information, or access to other professional or natural helping networks. The *level of willingness* to help is made explicit in the initial question asked of the central figure. However, once the organizer and the central figure begin linking specific names to specific capabilities and resources, the question invariably arises as to whether anyone will actually be willing to use those capabilities or resources to help.

For instance, a central figure who is unemployed and running short of money may be able to identify a brother who lives out of town who would be willing to loan him or her money and help in finding a job. Or the person may have an old friend whom he or she has not seen in years who now supervises an office or factory and who might be willing to give the central figure a job. This identification phase requires probing, encouragement, and support. It may also involve more than one or two sessions, particularly if the first identification phase and a follow-up fail to identify any potentially helpful network members.

Network Analysis. Network analysis, or mapping, is the second stage of personal networking. Once a list of network members has been developed and categorized on the basis of their relationship to the central figure (that is, relative, friend, neighbor, work colleague, or other), and once some measure of capabilities, resources, and willingness has been assessed, a limited personal or social network analysis is developed. Its purpose is to assess and identify quantitatively and, to a lesser extent, qualitatively, the strength of the dyadic ties in the network in order to maximize their effectiveness and efficiency while minimizing the amount of time or effort required of the network members. For some personal network members, it is not necessary to minimize their time or effort, and indeed it could even be counterproductive if a member is enthusiastic about helping, but it is necessary to avoid abusing that help.

The following network analysis factors need to be addressed in the second stage: frequency of contact, direction, duration, and intensity (which is a global measure of the tie). One commonly used network factor, density, is not as significant for the identification of analysis stages but is important in the linking stage.

Frequency of contact is simply how often the central figure is in contact with each network member by phone or in person. *Direction* refers to whether the central figure sees him- or herself as being in the past the giver of help or affection, the receiver, or as being equal or reciprocal. *Duration* refers to how long (in months or years) the members have known each other. *Intensity* refers to the degree of potential helpfulness or functionality and the degree of liking or affection that is felt toward the person.

Figure 4.4 gives an example of a clinical instrument that can be used to analyze a social network.

Linking. The most interesting, productive, and challenging part of personal networking now begins. It involves linking an individual up with the most appropriate primary network members, as listed in the Personal Networking Assessment Instrument. Both the networker and the individual he or she is helping may have only two or three names, or they may have thirty. Together, they must decide who to involve in helping and how to involve them.

Name, Address, and Telephone Number	Relationship (Relative, Friend, Neighbor, Work, Professional Helper or Other)	Willingness to Help (High, Medium, Low)	Capabilities Social/Emotional (briefly comment)	Resources Material/Contacts (briefly comment)	Frequency of Contact (Daily, Weekly, Bi-weekly, Monthly, Less)	Duration of Friendship (Month, 6 Mos., Year, 1-5 Years, Longer)	Intensity (Direction and Degree of Affection and Comfort -briefly comment)
1.							
2.							
3.							
4.							
5.							

Figure 4.4: Personal Networking Assessment Instrument

NETWORKING WITH INDIVIDUALS 79

The question of who to involve gradually becomes clearer as the networker goes over the instrument, particularly as he or she discusses the issues of willingness to help, capabilities, resources, and intensity of the relationship. As previously mentioned, there are ways of quantifying these variables much more precisely, but for personal networking purposes such quantification may be gained at the expense of practical understanding or clinical judgment. Instead, a thorough, empathic, supportive, problem-focused discussion of each and every network member should take place, the purpose of which should be how and if that person can help.

The discussion of how to involve people requires all of the areas on the instrument to be reviewed, as well as a discussion of such factors as who should approach them (as opposed to who should be approached), in what way, and at what time and place.

The networker is the intermediary between the individual and his or her network. It is preferable that the networker encourage the individual to make the contact with the network member, but this may be difficult or even inappropriate for some. This is particularly true for social isolates who may not have had any contact with family members for years. In some cases, a professional networker might be the best person to make the initial phone call to establish whether the relative or former friend is at all willing to help and to smooth the way for the individual.

When dealing with professional caregivers in the network, the professional might initially be able to negotiate with the network member better than the individual. For instance, with a health-related problem in which the individual or ego names a public health nurse as a potentially willing, capable, and resourceful person, a professional networker may be better able to present an argument to the local Department of Public Health for reopening the case immediately, whereas the individual alone would be more likely to be put on a waiting list.

The issue of how to involve a network member is the essence of linking. In discussions with the ego concerning who should be contacted, the networker will have eliminated those who are clearly unapproachable. The network members who are left need to be linked up by having the ego clearly and nondefensively explain the reason for the contact and the types of help needed.

Role playing frequently helps in instances where an ego is unsure of himself or herself, or unsure of how the network member will respond. Several scenarios should be used, starting with the most positive possible response, in which the network member enthusiastically responds that he or she can and will help and makes a firm commitment to do so. This should be followed by a more ambiguous role-playing scenario in which the ego has to convince the network member to help. Finally, a situation in which the network member refuses to help should be rehearsed with a subsequent discussion between the networker and the ego concerning options.

Time and place are also practical concerns in relation to how to link up with network members. For social-emotional issues between relatives and friends, the best time is the evening at their home. For material resources or contacts with professional caregivers or work associates, the best link-up place is the work setting during the daytime. It is as inappropriate and counterproductive to call a relative or friend at work during the day as it is to call a professional who is not a friend at his or her home in the evening.

Let us look at some examples:

Example 1. A 34-year-old woman presented herself at a family and social service agency saying that she was feeling depressed and overwhelmed. She had a five-year-old boy and an eight-year-old girl whom she was raising alone since her divorce two years ago. Between working as a waitress and raising her family, she had virtually no social life or recreation, and she was feeling that she was overly harsh on her children and seemed to be taking her anger and frustration out on them. She knew the agency ran a good, free summer recreation program for children, and she had heard from a friend that she could come there and talk with a social worker to get some help and advice.

I spoke with her and established that her depression was clearly a reaction to the situation and well within the normal range. After allowing her to ventilate and explain her problem and situation, I suggested networking.

In the second session, after explaining individual networking to this somewhat skeptical woman, I helped her diagram her social network, as explained in Chapter 1. This led to some discussion of the people involved, as well as a noticeable improvement in her affect as she discussed three potentially helpful members. This completed stage one and got us well into stage two. At the third session, we went over the Personal Networking Assessment Instrument while focusing on the resources and capabilities of three central members.

The three significant network members who seemed to be the most potentially useful to this woman were her sister, her mother, and her closest friend. Each of them had different capabilities and access to different resources. Both the mother and the sister were willing to provide more child care than the woman had requested, and it was decided to take advantage of that resource. Her closest friend was also divorced but was dating and had an active social life. This friend enthusiastically agreed to introduce her to several members of her own network of friends who tended to be a reasonably homogeneous group of women who socialized together. This second-order network also had multiple linkages to other individuals and activities. For instance, some of these women were members of a volleyball team, one wanted to play tennis regularly (as did the client), and one was in a church choir.

The client, with my active encouragement, support, and guidance, became involved in all of these activities. As she became less depressed and overwhelmed through treatment and the gradual increase in her developing network, she gained the confidence to join her closest friend for a double date. Furthermore, she developed the confidence through these social supports to get back in touch with her ex-husband. He was not helpful as a social support, and reconciliation was not considered useful by her, but she had never worked through her intense anger toward him. Her new network, which consisted now of four other divorced or separated women, strongly encouraged her to confront him, not only for the purpose of ventilation, but also for clarification of what had caused their break-up. It had become clear that part of her depression was based on self-blame for the divorce. That self-blame was misdirected, and by sharing her experiences and trauma with this new network of friends and then, in turn, hearing about their similar problems, she was helped immensely.

Individual networking is not appropriate for everyone, but there are few instances in the field of social work where this type of linking cannot be useful. Whether dealing with cases of severe individual or family psychopathology, or helping individuals find new jobs, the planned and systematic utilization of actual and potential social networks will prove to be useful.

Networkers must be sensitive to both the strengths and the limitations of relevant networks. They cannot provide treatment for serious emotional problems (only a well-trained professional can do that), but they can immeasurably support any treatment gains and provide an environment or ecology that frequently makes the difference between the ultimate success or failure of therapeutic interventions in the finding and development of resources and jobs. This point is well established in the innovative work of Germain and Gitterman (1980) in their "life model" or ecological approach to social work practice, as well as in other ecologically sensitive approaches utilizing groups (Balgopal and Vassil, 1983). As research further clarifies the configurations and purposes of networks, and as other networking and ecological approaches are developed and tested, social workers will find themselves increasingly in the role of networkers.

REFERENCES

BALGOPAL, P. R. and T. V. VASSIL (1983) Groups in Social Work: An Ecological Perspective. New York: Macmillan.

CAMPBELL, A., D. E. CONVERSE, and W. L. RODGERS (1976) The Quality of American Life. New York: Russell Sage Foundation.

CAPLAN, G. (1974) Support Systems and Community Mental Health. New York: Behavioral.

CRAVEN, P. and B. WELLMAN (1973) "The network city." Sociological Inquiry 43: 57-88.

DEAN, A. and N. LIN (1977) "The stress-buffering role of social support: problems and prospects for systematic investigation." Journal of Nervous and Mental Disease 165: 403-417.

FARIS, R. E. and W. H. DUNHAM (1939) Mental Disorders in Urban Areas. Chicago: University of Chicago Press.

FISCHER, C., R. JACKSON, C. STUEVE, K. GERSON, and L. JONES (1977) Networks and Places. New York: Free Press.

GERMAIN, C. B. and A. GITTERMAN (1980) The Life Model of Social Work Practice. New York: Columbia University Press.

GOTTLIEB, B. (1981) "Preventive intervention involving social networks and social support," in B. Gottlieb (ed.) Social Networks and Social Support. Beverly Hills, CA: Sage.

GURIN, G., J. VEROFF, and S. FELD (1960) Americans View Their Mental Health. New York: Basic Books.

KULKA, R., J. VEROFF, and E. DOUVAIN (1979) "Social class and the use of professional help for personal problems: 1957 and 1976." Journal of Health and Social Behavior 20: 2-17.

LEE, N. H. (1969) The Search for an Abortionist. Chicago: University of Chicago Press.

MAGUIRE, L. (1980) "The interface of social workers with personal networks." Social Work with Groups 3 (Fall): 39-49.

SROLE, L., T. S. LANGNER, S. T. MICHAEL, P. KIRKPATRICK, M. K. OPLER, and T.A.C. RENNIE (1975) Mental Health in the Metropolis (2 vols.) New York: Harper & Row.

WELLMAN, B. (1981) "Applying network analysis to the study of support," in B. Gottlieb (ed.) Social Networks and Social Support. Beverly Hills, CA: Sage.

Chapter 5

SELF-HELP GROUPS

Self-help groups are included in a book dealing with networks because many of the groups develop from natural networks of friends who share a concern or problem. Furthermore, the differences between self-help and mutual aid groups, as opposed to naturally developed networks, consist primarily in the depth of formal organization rather than any more essential characteristics. In short, self-help groups are networks of people who consciously define membership, goals, and purposes, whereas most natural networks are groups of people with shifting memberships and no explicit and conscious purpose for existing.

Another similarity is the way they develop. Networks develop and communicate through a series of links between people. These linkages are based on knowledge of each other and/or some shared interests and concerns. Self-help groups develop in the same way. The difference is that the self-help group will formally convene or meet en masse as a single entity to corroborate their linkages, connections, and common concerns. The naturally developed network remains more fluid and is unlikely to actually meet face to face as a group at any one time.

Regardless of how self-help groups develop, they all have relatively clearly defined goals in mind. These self-help group goals may involve:

(1) raising money (for example, the March of Dimes or the American Cancer Society);
(2) political/social action (for example, the Gay Caucus, most neighborhood organizations, the National Organization for Women—NOW);

(3) consciousness raising (for example, the many women's groups that meet to support each other, often referring to themselves as "networks");

(4) mutual aid and support (for example, Recovery Incorporated, Alcoholics Anonymous, Candlelighters).

Self-help groups have flourished in the past few years. Their numbers and types have been developing at such a rapid pace that it is now very difficult to estimate how many exist or precisely what they do. Some estimate their number at three-quarters of a million groups in the United States, with a membership of over 15 million (Langton and Petersen, 1982). Due to their diversity, the lack of a clear, agreed upon definition of the term, and the informal, nonprofessional, and therefore "nonmonitored" status of the groups, any estimates concerning the size of this movement is only guesswork. However, it undeniably includes a great many people and appears to be growing.

The fact that so many different types of self-help groups exist has made them difficult to define or classify. Many, however, have attempted to do so even though self-help groups vary immensely in their organization, development, and purpose. They can be seen as social or political movements trying to change society, or as treatment for the emotional pain of individuals. They are used as a means to educate the masses about health or welfare problems, or they may be highly secretive, distant clusters of people who choose to isolate themselves from the rest of society. Some seek publicity for their cause, while others avoid it. Killilea (1976) notes that self-help groups have been seen as social systems, social movements, spiritual movements, secular religions, consumer participant systems, alternative caregiving systems, intentional communities, subcultural ways of life, supplementary communities, expressive social influence groups, and as organizations for the deviant and stigmatized.

Another very thorough typology has been developed (Langton and Petersen, 1982) which distinguishes them on the basis of their purpose and issue areas. The purposes of self-help groups can include fellowship, education, advocacy, and direct service. Relevant issues include health, economic development, community development/housing, human services/education, and consumer issues. By drawing a simple grid, with the different purposes comprising the column on the left and the different issues comprising the top row, one can distinguish the different types reasonably well.

Caplan (1974) refers to three different purposes of self-help groups. The first of these is the group dedicated to helping people through transitions, or where there has been rapid cultural change or social disorganization. Examples of such groups include ethnic organizations, as well as veterans' groups. People who have suffered disabilities or undergone difficult experiences and bond together to provide mutual support to overcome mutual problems comprise the second type of self-help group, which Caplan refers to as "Collective Anologues" of people, or specialized caregivers. Alcoholics Anonymous is an example of this. A third type of self-help group is that which provides a new community in which members can involve themselves. Parents Without Partners is an example of just such a group.

It is generally conceded that self-help groups do have in common the following characteristics: (1) they involve face-to-face contact or minimally a phone-to-phone network; (2) they are self-reliant, although some rely on a national organization for some financial or administrative support; (3) they have in common an identifiable problem, concern, or social-cultural heritage; (4) they tend to be grass-roots movements that develop spontaneously, usually to fill a perceived need; and (5) they emphasize reliance on the self-help group itself rather than on any agency, organization, or formal system maintained by professionals. However, as we will see later in this chapter, there are many ways for professionals to work with them.

Their purposes or goals frequently tend to involve the provision of support for people with a shared concern. Thus friendship, community, mutual guidance and advice, and a general caring and concern displayed for other members is fairly uniform. More specific purposes are necessarily defined as a function of the particular shared purpose of the group. For instance, in Alcoholics Anonymous the goal is to maintain sobriety or abstinence for recovering alcoholics, while other self-help groups seek to change certain legislation, provide a growth stimulus or consciousness-raising experience for women, men, minorities, and so on, or even to provide peer psychotherapy or guidance.

The purposes of self-help groups clearly coincide with those of professionally developed groups. Caplan's three self-help group purposes provide an example. Social group workers frequently work with transitional groups of clients adjusting to retirement or divorce, or of clients returning to their communities from hospitals. Social workers have traditionally been the leaders in working with immigrant groups as they learn to survive and cope in this country, as well as with those who have suffered due to social disorganization caused by changing neighborhoods and the changing roles and values of one's family.

The second sort of self-help group, composed of people who share a common problem or disability, has likewise been a mainstay of the profession. Whether in hospital settings or social service agencies, social workers have long facilitated and developed groups that are composed of people who share a common disability such as alcoholism, high blood pressure, or a defined psychiatric disorder.

The last type of group, that which provides a "new community" of sorts, is less commonly perceived as a professional social group worker's function and has, in fact, a long-standing tradition within self-help movements. This area has not traditionally been seen as a social group worker's "territory."

The reason for the development of self-help and mutual aid groups is very similar to that of networks. In fact, basically all of the reasons for the rise in the use of networking, as stated in the last chapter, apply to self-help groups as well. Quite simply, people prefer to go to their own friends, relatives, neighbors, and anyone else with whom they have a personal relationship and whom they trust. The bond that exists between and among friends and relatives is based on genuine concern for one another. However, when we speak of small, face-to-face self-help or mutual aid groups, the tie or bond that actually influences change is based on several unique properties (Lieberman, 1979). Regardless of the group's ideologies, leadership, basis for organization, or even its members' particular affliction, they see certain qualities as being significant to the help they seek in joining the group.

The most important of these is the feeling of belonging (Lieberman, 1979). This refers to a shared feeling of similarly afflicted people that develops into cohesiveness. In short, because people feel they belong in the group, the group becomes more cohesive, accepting, and supportive of its members. This feeling brings them together into a tight unit, microcosm, or social system in which they are no longer deviant or even alone in their suffering, but rather are members of an almost familylike system.

This belonging is actually reinforced by the deviancy of the group. Their bond is based on being different—a clear recognition of the "us-them" situation. This separateness, based on being different from the rest of society, may isolate them in some way from others. They perceive this isolation from society as already existing even without the group, but it also helps to develop the group's bond or cohesiveness. The self-help group member's behavior thus becomes partially controlled by this supportive, cohesive bond.

Conformity to the group's way of thinking and acting develops. Very dense groups develop a clearly discernible system of rewards and punishments that has an extremely strong effect on those members who value their membership highly. Their attitudes, beliefs, and behavior will all change, if necessary, to conform to the belief system of the group (Yalom, 1976). This conformity may have positive as well as negative effects.

Another quality of self-help groups that influences change is their capacity to produce major affective states or to have a highly emotional impact on an individual. Most notable in groups such as Compassionate Friends are the feelings of pain, anger, and profound sadness, especially at their opening ritual at which they recite the loss of a child. These strong emotions are shared, built, and developed among the members. These strong feelings and expressions of emotion bring them together and make them into a cohesive group. This kind of cathartic experience has been a mainstay of professionals since Freud and works no less effectively in self-help groups.

Finally, the last factor that affects a self-help group's ability to change is the fact that it provides a basis for social comparison. The members share and compare their attitudes and feelings with those of others. In so doing, they learn new ways of feeling about themselves, their problem or concern, and their social situation.

Levy (1979) statistically analyzed a number of the activities of several self-help groups and noted that the nine most frequently occurring activities were empathy, mutual affirmation, explanation, sharing, morale-building, self-disclosure, positive reinforcement, personal goal-setting, and catharsis. It is interesting to note that these efforts, which can be generally described as ways of fostering communication, providing social support, and responding to members' needs on both the cognitive and emotional levels, are in contrast to professionally run therapeutic groups. Levy points out that the least frequently encountered activities in self-help groups are far more likely to be encountered in the "artificial" settings of group psychotherapists. These activities include confrontation, punishment, requesting feedback, behavioral rehearsal, offering feedback, extinction, modeling, reference to group norms, and behavioral proscription. Levy sees the self-help group setting as far more natural and comparable to routine but supportive interactions, and suggests that this fact would therefore require less readjustment and induce less stress than professionally run groups.

Once we start comparing services, as many have done (Powell, 1977, 1982; Lieberman and Borman, 1979; Levy, 1979), we must address the issue of "territory," or professional domain, which is in fact an underlying concern of many. While it may be impolitic to address the issue directly, it may be even more hazardous to avoid it. Social group workers in many instances have already developed excellent working relationships with self-help groups and have found that their ties with them enhance their own work with clients immensely. Increasingly, social workers are finding and developing ways of interrelating with self-help groups and movements without "taking them over" and thus undermining those very potent curative factors of altruism and acceptance by peers that seem to be intrinsic to self-help groups. They are also finding that the former hostility (or at least what many of us were led to believe would be hostility) is no longer there, or at least is not universal. In fact, many self-help groups now rely heavily on professionals to assist them in various ways.

As the interface between social group workers and self-help groups becomes more routinized and common, past prejudices and misconceptions will no doubt diminish and the issue of "territory" should become a moot point as mutual assistance, support, and referral interchanges develop. Most prejudices tend to diminish with time, contact, and involvement.

However, a second hindrance to this mutual help between professionals and self-help groups may not go away without more research. That hindrance exists in the misconception that self-help groups are not helpful and may in fact do harm. While the definitive study of their effectiveness has yet to be done (a statement that can be made of any social work or human endeavor), Lieberman and Borman's (1979) work does indicate that they may be quite helpful. Although outcome measures are difficult to develop, self-help groups apparently do no harm and may in fact be helpful in some respects for women's consciousness-raising groups (CR), Mended Hearts (a self-help group for recovering heart attack patients), and SAGE (the Senior Actualization and Growth Encounter group for the elderly). Results were quite mixed, however, and indicated that, for instance, while CR groups for women can play a helpful role therapeutically as an adjunct for women already in treatment, they had no significant impact on symptom distress, coping styles, or marital relationships. They did, however, help women to reassess themselves, with the frequent result of increased self-esteem, renewed self-respect, and an acknowledgment of their own self-importance (Lieberman et al., 1979).

However, several instances of poorly handled terminations were cited that professionally trained social group workers would presumably have managed quite differently and more effectively. Additional outcome research comparing self-help to treatment groups has been done in relation to Alcoholics Anonymous, concluding that AA is at least as effective as most other treatments of alcoholism (Armor et al., 1976). Thus, while well-controlled comparative studies with a sufficient number of subjects are lacking, it seems that self-help groups do at least fill a certain social-emotional need for some people. In fairness to both professionally developed groups and self-help groups, it would seem that adequate comparative research is simply inconclusive, and it cannot therefore be stated that any one is superior to the other overall.

Finally, before examining the ways in which a networker can work with the self-help groups in a given community, a word of caution is in order. It may be useful to recall some of the countertherapeutic excesses of the late 1960s and early 1970s in relation to nonprofessional encounter groups. While many professionals were also remiss, it appeared that the negative effects of the encounter groups were at least partially a function of the lack of training or awareness of psychopathology (or even "normal" human behavior and development) on the part of many of the nonprofessional group leaders (Lieberman et al., 1973). There are already problems in the self-help movement concerning poorly timed or counterproductive confrontations. Professionalism or a graduate degree in social work may not be the answer, but better communication and trust, combined with a mutual exchange of ideas, as well as clients, would seem to be appropriate for the two systems. This leads us directly into the two major ways in which networkers can work effectively with self-help groups. The models are the Clearinghouse Model and the Developer/Facilitator Model, each of which has several variations.

CLEARINGHOUSE MODEL

One way to network on the macro level, for the purpose of helping a city or large town, is by locating and coordinating self-help groups. Ultimately, the goal is twofold: to develop a directory of all the self-help groups in the area and to form a network of such groups. One can proceed with this model using three stages: identification, directory development, and linking (Maguire, 1983).

STAGE I

This first stage involves basic networking techniques, namely, calling and writing to the relevant professionals and nonprofessionals in the community who may have contact with or knowledge of the existence of self-help groups.

One can begin by calling one's own network members, that is, those with whom one has a personal or professional relationship, and asking them for the names of other professionals and self-help group leaders. This primary network will consist of fellow social workers, nurses, psychologists, and doctors, as well as self-help group leaders whom one may already know. Next, inform them of the goal of networking for a clearinghouse in which one will identify self-help groups in your locale, develop a directory of them, and finally link them up through an ongoing network, as well as through one's own continued information and referral service for the education of professionals and the public.

One's own effectiveness and credibility will be enhanced by being on the staff of an active, visible, and respected community-oriented agency. I have helped to do this in Pittsburgh through the Information and Volunteer Services Agency and its Volunteer Action Center, as well as through the School of Social Work. Leonard Borman performed a similar service in the Chicago area through the auspices of private foundation funding and a university, and on Long Island and New York it was done through a Family and Children's Social Service Agency.

After one has personally contacted the primary network members, the secondary network members need to be contacted. These comprise both professionals and self-help leaders known to the primary network members, and about whom one may know something, but whom one does not know personally.

For instance, a networker may not know the Alcoholics Anonymous leaders, but he or she knows that they exist in the community. Their contact person, as well as the leaders of other major self-help groups that may have several chapters locally, need to be contacted. One can learn how to contact them by referring to Gartner and Riessman's *Help: A Working Guide to Self-Help Groups* (1981), or by contacting the National Self-Help Clearinghouse at 33 West 42nd Street, New York, New York 10036 (212/840-7606).

STAGE II: DIRECTORY DEVELOPMENT

This stage involves the development of a self-help directory by writing and calling the second-order network to inform them of one's networking intentions and to ask them for information. The information being gathered will include:

(1) name, telephone number, and address of organization;
(2) group goals and purposes;
(3) membership criteria (that is, whether it is limited to only the widowed, or alcoholics, or arthritics, and so forth);
(4) fees or dues;
(5) meeting formats or how meetings are conducted (Are there lectures, do people give vignettes or testimonies? and so on);
(6) meeting times and places (This is optional and should be exluded if they change every few months); and
(7) sponsorship or professional involvement (that is, does a church community group or social service agency help them, and are professionals involved in any capacity?).

This directory development stage requires that one gather the necessary information systematically, put it into a book or otherwise centralize it in one's own office, and then get the word out to the public and professionals.

STAGE III: LINKING

This stage involves informing and educating the public and professionals about the self-help groups. I have received help from the public relations staff at the university, as well as from Information and Volunteer Services and contacts with the local newspapers, radio, and TV. They advertised two different conferences that got self-help group leaders and professionals together to share ideas and concerns. These conferences consisted of panels and presentations by self-help group leaders and professionals on such topics as self-help and professionals, recruiting members, running groups, and death and dying.

Such conferences require a great deal of free time where self-help members and professionals can get together over a meal or coffee and talk about mutual interests and concerns. Much of the distance that still exists between professionals and self-help groups is due to a lack of this linking process. Networkers need to develop those linkages to establish an environment in which professionals and self-help leaders get to know each other personally, as equals, with different capabilities to offer the community.

Another way of encouraging this linkage is through a fair. Once one has the names of what one believes to be most of the self-help groups in one's community, one should use any available media help (see Silverman, 1980, for some excellent ideas regarding the media) to advertise a fair. A Self-Help Fair is composed of booths and tables at which professionals and self-help groups pass out literature and make themselves available to each other and the public to answer questions. Other parts of a program, such as panels, presentations, or demonstrations are also encouraged in order to attract people.

The linking process can also be developed by establishing an ongoing self-help network. Monthly meetings may be sufficient. Even though, as a networker, one may hope to see a more dense network of such self-help groups, it has been my experience that the idea of such groups is simply not a sufficient motivator for most, particularly for self-help leaders themselves. Their interest and focus lie in their particular problem area, whether that is alcoholism, diabetes, or a cause. Their identification and loyalty are to the group, not to a clearinghouse network or a concept called self-help.

Finally, a speakers' bureau might be set up composed of self-help leaders and professionals. These speakers would be volunteers from the clearinghouse network who support the idea of developing self-help groups.

In some instances, one may have requests from self-help groups asking for a professional such as a doctor to speak to their group about the effects of alcohol or drugs. In other instances, one may get requests from professionals asking for a representative from a self-help group to explain their goals and the way they work with people.

In this clearinghouse model, the networker will be constantly trying to educate the community and link up appropriate parties. The networker needs to identify the self-help resources, both professional and nonprofessional, organize those resources into a clear directory (or at least centralize them into a clearinghouse office for information and referral), and link those resources together into a mutual supportive network.

DEVELOPER/FACILITATOR MODEL

There are a variety of ways in which networkers can work with self-help groups. Silverman (1980) distinguishes between those who work through agencies, such as professionals, and nonprofessional self-help leaders. The types of things that they can do with self-help groups are different.

The nonprofessional who joins because he or she shares a particular problem or concern is motivated by a desire to give and receive help from similarly afflicted people or others who share a strong concern about some issue. The fellow members of the group identify with this person, and a bond of trust and friendship may develop, based on sharing and reciprocity.

A professional often has the advantage of training and knowledge about either group dynamics or development, or about the particular disease, problem, or concern. This knowledge engenders respect in the group and puts him or her in a leadership position.

There are also disadvantages for both. Some self-help leaders find themselves frequently vying for control or authority over the group, since they have no credentials for this position. They also tend to blame themselves and get discouraged when things do not go well, leading to the incredibly high failure rate of such groups. Not knowing the many problems related to group dynamics and development, they often see the group's failure to get off the ground as a personal failure, a problem that is somewhat less likely among professionals. Furthermore, there are other serious disadvantages in that such techniques as blaming the victim, encouragement of a denial of certain emotions, preaching, and "pep talks" are all frequently and inappropriately used by self-help group leaders. Most professionals know better as a result of their education.

On the other hand, professionals are disadvantaged either by their attitudes or their education. Attitudinally, it is difficult for some to let nonprofessionals run their own group. I have had graduate students tell me that their self-help group was having trouble separating from them. I suspect that this is usually a two way street.

Gartner and Riessman (1981) suggest a sort of gradual disengagement for professionals. They refer to the "organizer" in much the same way as I refer to a networker, and see this person as taking three different roles as the group progresses. At first, the organizer needs to be a *catalyst*. That person identifies potential members, sets the meeting time and place, conducts meetings, explains self-help concepts, and assists members in getting to know one another. Gradually, the organizer moves into the less active role of *technical assistant*. In this role, he or she is not an active group member, but rather observes the group and provides it with feedback, encouragement, support, and suggestions. Finally, the organizer serves only as a *resource member,* responding to the group whenever they require it, but no longer being very actively involved.

Silverman (1980) suggests that professionals can interact with mutual help groups in at least four ways: by making referrals, by serving on advisory boards, by serving as consultants to existing groups, and by helping to develop new groups. Most of her excellent book, entitled *Mutual Help Groups: Organization and Development,* deals with the last issue.

I have recommended yet another way for professionals to work with self-help groups that is more in line with the networking concept (Maguire, 1981). My approach is based on several experiences, but one in particular on the Pine Ridge Indian Reservation in South Dakota.

A client of mine was married to a man who was very active in the community. He had lived off the reservation for many years and had been an alcoholic. He joined AA and credited it for saving him. This man had tried on many occasions to set up an AA chapter on the reservation but had been unable to do so. In many discussions that I had with him over the years, I agreed to aid in developing and facilitating his work by providing him with certain resources that would enable him to get an AA group started without undermining its self-help principles. I have since used these same resources to start other self-help groups.

Some important resources that can be provided by professionals are:

(1) *Meeting Place.* Many self-help groups either failed quickly or never got developed due to the lack of a good place to meet. Hospitals, clinics, social service agencies, churches, and community organizations all have meeting rooms that are generally free in the evenings. One could develop self-help groups by linking them up with these professional or community resources to provide a place to meet.

(2) *Financial support.* Self-help is a comparatively cheap way of providing and receiving help, yet even it needs some funds. The financial support needed is minimal and can usually be supplied in the form of coffee for the first few meetings, secretarial help, postage stamps, and the use of a telephone. In most instances, one can arrange for oneself or one's agency to be reimbursed once the group gets started.

(3) *Information.* One can assist by telling self-help group leaders about related resources or benefits. For instance, if one is a social worker trying to assist a self-help group of widows, one may get them information from the social security office or from legal aid about their benefits.

(4) *Training.* This resource involves providing useful, complementary education or skill development for group members or leaders. For instance, Mended Hearts, which is a mutual aid group of people with heart disorders, may want someone to come in and train them in Cardiopulmonary Resuscitation (CPR), or a group may want a professional to come in and discuss group development or recruiting for membership. The training is not designed to make them into professionals, but rather to enable them to improve their own aid to each other.

(5) *Referrals to Self-Help Groups.* If one has personal contacts with self-help leaders and makes referrals to them, the groups are far more likely to succeed. Over half the members of the first AA chapter on the reservation were referrals made by me. The rest were people who came because they heard about it from their own network of relatives and friends or were referred by other professionals.

(6) *Referrals from Self-Help Groups.* Networkers often find that as they develop relationships with self-help groups, members will be referred to them for treatment or help. The fear on the part of some professionals that self-help groups will compete with them for clients is not only unjustified, but just the opposite is true. I found that the community mental health center gradually became inundated with clients who were AA members and had also been told to come in and talk with me about their problems. It became a mutual referral system that ultimately was an extremely beneficial factor in the community.

(7) *Credibility in the Community.* It helps to make one's work known within the nonprofessional community. Various community action groups and leaders are frequently either ignorant of the existence of various groups or of their goals and purposes. In one's work with them, or even in social gatherings, it helps to publicize one's involvement because of the frequent biases against self-help groups. On the reservation, several community leaders indicated that they believed that AA meetings were just excuses

for alcoholics to meet and drink together. My subsequent discussions with them and the fact of my aid to the groups changed that perception.

(8) *Credibility Among Professionals.* A lack of knowledge and frequent misperceptions about self-help groups are also prevelant among professionals. In my work, medical doctors have been particularly singled out for their lack of knowledge or support of self-help groups for arthritics, diabetics, stroke victims, and other health-related problems. One will find that by mentioning various self-help groups at case conferences or rounds, or at professional conferences, one will pique the curiosity (and occasional animosity) of other social workers, doctors, nurses, and counselors, which allows one the opportunity to do some educating and make the groups more "acceptable" to our more rigid professional brethren.

(9) *Buffer.* One will find that occasionally self-help groups come under attack from other professionals, family members, community residents, or friends of members. These attacks may consist of charges of cruel actions on the part of the group (such as confronting an alcoholic spouse with his or her problem) or, more subtly, of "alienation of affection." Some of this criticism is justified and some is not, but a networker may sometimes need to serve as an outside buffer or even critic under certain circumstances. One may be called on to meet with a critical professional or family member, assess the charge objectively, and then provide appropriate feedback to both the group and the person with the complaint.

(10) *Social and Emotional Support.* After many years of education and experience with groups, I am still unable to get more than one-third of them developed satisfactorily. I no longer take this personally, but most self-help group leaders do and inappropriately tend to blame themselves or others. Professionals have supervisors or professors to provide feedback and give them the needed social and emotional support to know when and how to change their approach, or when to give up. Networkers must provide that support and guidance to self-help leaders.

This chapter on self-help groups has reviewed some of the ways and reasons that self-help and mutual aid groups develop. The current upsurge of interest in these groups is the result of many of the same factors that have made networking so popular. These include the economy, a disenchantment with professionals and experts, a perception of inefficiency and ineffectiveness within the formal or professional sector, and the fact of success building on success in the self-help movement. Their dynamics and developmental processes are seen as very similar to those of professionally developed groups, although there are certain distinct differences.

Networking with self-help groups can take many forms. One may serve as a clearinghouse or information and referral networker, or actually develop and run groups until it is time to gradually disengage, or one can provide certain specific resources to a group and its leaders to enable them to start on their own.

REFERENCES

ARMOR, D., J. POLICH, and H. STAMBUL (1976) Alcoholism and Treatment. Santa Monica, CA: Rand Corporation.

CAPLAN, G. (1974) Support Systems and Community Mental Health. New York: Behavioral.

GARTNER, F. and A. RIESSMAN (1981) Help: A Working Guide to Self-Help Groups. New York: New Viewpoint Books.

KILLILEA, M. (1976) "Mutual help organizations: interpretations in the literature," in G. Caplan and M. Killilea (eds.) Support Systems and Mutual Help: Multidisciplinary Explorations. New York: Grune & Stratton.

LANGTON, S. and J. PETERSEN (1982) "What is self-help?" Citizen Participation 3 (January/February).

LEVY, L. (1979) "Processes and activities in groups," in M. Liebermann and L. Borman (eds.) Self-Help Groups for Coping with Crisis. San Francisco: Jossey-Bass.

LIEBERMAN, M. A. (1979) "Analyzing change mechanisms in groups," in M. A. Lieberman and L. Borman (eds.) Self-Help Groups for Coping with Crisis. San Francisco: Jossey-Bass.

——— and L. BORMAN (1979) Self-Help Groups for Coping with Crisis. San Francisco: Jossey-Bass.

LIEBERMAN, M., I. D. YALOM, and M. B. MILES (1973) Encounter Groups: First Facts. New York: Basic Books.

LIEBERMAN, M., G. R. Bond, N. SOLOW, and J. RIEBSTEIN (1979) "Effectiveness of women's consciousness raising," in M. Lieberman and L. Borman (eds.) Self-Help Groups for Coping with Crisis. San Francisco: Jossey-Bass.

MAGUIRE, L. (1983) "Networking for self-help: an empirically based perspective," in F. Cox et al. (eds.) Tactics and Techniques of Community Practice (2nd ed.). Itasca, IL: Peacock.

——— (1981) "Natural helping networks and self-help groups," in M. Nobel (ed.) Primary Prevention in Mental Health and Social Work: New York: Council on Social Work Education.

POWELL, T. (1981) "Impact of social networks on help-seeking behavior." Social Work 26 (July): 335-337.

——— (1977) "Comparisons between self-help groups and professional services." Social Casework 60 (November): 561-565.

SILVERMAN, P. (1980) Mutual Help Groups: Organization and Development. Beverly Hills, CA: Sage.

YALOM, I. (1976) The Theory and Practice of Group Psychotherapy (2nd ed.). New York: Basic Books.

Chapter 6

NETWORKING WITH ORGANIZATIONS

Human service organizations grew at a tremendous rate during the 1960s and early 1970s. In certain areas, that growth has continued to accelerate, with dramatic effects. However, it has been financed by the public and by politicians whose long-term loyalty to sound and consistent programs and services is rather suspect.

What is needed is a way to combine certain services and programs so that overlap is minimized and the most cost-efficient and effective use of services maintained. A way is needed to connect the many service providers and their organizations into a single unit that is densely intertwined, so that each can communicate and share resources while still maintaining its own special focus. We have once again defined networking, but this time at an organizational level.

The need for better communication and resource-sharing is fairly obvious among people who have worked in social service agencies, mental health clinics, hospitals, legal aid offices, employment offices, and a wide variety of other health and welfare offices. If a divorced, depressed, unemployed single parent presents him- or herself at a legal aid office, he or she will be helped by a lawyer or a paraprofessional to deal with divorce settlement issues. If that same person goes to a community mental health center, he or she will be seen by a social worker, psychiatrist, or psychologist and helped with depression, if necessary. If he or she goes to the state unemployment office or a vocational rehabilitation office, the person will be seen by counselors to help get a new job or learn new skills. If the person goes to a self-help group for single parents, he or she will be helped by others to cope with the problems of being a single parent.

There is often no particular order or logic to how or why people choose one type of organization over another. It is usually a function of their own perception of whatever is of the greatest importance among their myriad problems. This decision is also very much a result of the availability of certain resources, of the individual's knowledge of those services, and of their own history and how they have learned to cope with problems in the past. Let us look at each of these factors: perception, availability, knowledge, and coping strategies.

One's perception or frame of mind or reference is the most important factor in a person's decision of where to turn for help. It is difficult to divorce the purely subjective from the objective factors here, but basically we are referring to whether a person thinks in "legalistic," "psychological," or a type of "problem-solving" way, as weighted by the urgency of some aspect of their problem. For instance, if our multiproblem person tends to think in legalistic terms, and has just learned that his or her spouse is suing to take the children, the person would probably perceive the problem as a legal one requiring the services of a lawyer.

If the person has a more psychological frame of reference and feels that he or she can do nothing until overcoming his or her overwhelming depression, the person will probably go to a clinical social worker or psychologist first.

If a person's unemployment benefits have run out and he or she needs to pay the rent, due tomorrow, and if his or her usual frame of reference is a practical, problem-solving method, the person may seek out a staff person at the state welfare office who is familiar with the job market and/or financial benefits that may be available.

Availability has to be considered almost simultaneously in this process, because if the type of help a person is seeking is not available or is not known to the person, it does him or her no good. Furthermore, one's history of involvement with organizations and one's idiosyncratic way of coping and working through problems all come into play.

This decision-making process on the part of a person seeking help is highly complex and inefficient. There are often so many factors to be considered and so little available knowledge that people end up going to a service-provider whose focus is very limited.

Unfortunately, the same types of problems exist among the service-providers as among the service-seekers. Psychiatrists see people's problems as being psychiatric or related to thought disturbance, anxiety, depression, or a wide range of mental health disorders. Social workers perceive the problems of people in terms of their social-environmental context, particularly in relation to family, group, or interpersonal relationships. Lawyers perceive most problems as being related to a client's rights in regard to the law and the legal system. For each profession, the provider who feels that he or she has the time available to help, the particular kind of knowledge or information needed, as well as some experience in working with this particular type of person will take the case.

Essentially, we have two fragmented systems heading toward each other in a haphazard fashion. Perhaps this is as it should be and must be attributed to human nature. We cannot dictate to those seeking help where they can go, nor can we tell providers precisely whom they may and may not help. Even establishing precise, clear guidelines would be difficult, given both the tremendous overlap of needs on the part of each person seeking help, as well as the overlap of services provided. However, some order could be brought to this process by developing and using certain networking principles within organizations. This is by no means a new or radical suggestion, and it has already been successfully tried by many. Networking in organizations can be done on the micro level for individual clients or patients, in which case it is generally referred to as case management, or it can be done on a macro level, in which case it is called human service organization networking.

CASE MANAGEMENT NETWORKING

Variations of this approach have been around for many years under the name of the "team approach" or "case coordination." It involves teams or networks of professionals working together to pool their talents and resources in order to help a single client or patient work through his or her problem. They are typically developed either within large, multiservice organizations or among several different organizations. Their membership and functions vary with the type of client or problem presented. Curtis (1981) clearly delineated the "actors" potentially involved in a case management approach, as evidenced in Figure 6.1.

Most large social service agencies or community mental health centers can work quite successfully through case management. For instance, if an anxious adolescent girl comes into a large community mental health center, she will first be seen by an intake worker. This worker evaluates the problem, writes up a case history and a tentative diagnosis or problem statement, and then refers the case to a multidisciplinary team. The team is typically composed of a psychiatrist and/or a psychologist, plus one or more social workers, nurses, and other counselors. One person from that team will then be assigned the role of case manager based on whoever's services are needed most. The case manager's task is to insure that the client receives all of the necessary services needed, assuming that all cases have multifaceted problems. In some instances, the team itself will have

Actors (row and column headings) and
Focus (cells) of Case Management
Developed by W. R. Curtis

Being Managed	Doing Management			
	self	paraprofessional	professional worker	managers
client	self-help	advocate/helper	clinical services	client pathway
family	mutual care	social services	social services	family policy
social network	mutual care		problem-solving in a social network	creating opportunities for differentiation
community	local government	prevention	prevention	community development
professionals	professional self-management	case management system	interdisciplinary team	management information system

Source: Curtis, 1981

Figure 6.1: Actors and Focus of Case Management

staff designated as case managers (often a position requiring less than a master's degree). These people will assume no direct treatment responsibility, but will instead serve to connect the client with the needed direct service staff within the agency.

If the aforementioned adolescent is sexually active and fearful of becoming pregnant, she may be assigned to a psychiatric nurse as the case manager and primary counselor. This nurse may then link the girl up with a social worker who will see her and her family together for several sessions.

If an alcoholic, sixty-year-old, depressed single male comes into a community health clinic and is assigned a case manager by an intake worker, a similar networking process will ensue, but with different links or anchorage points in the network. In this instance, a specialist in drug and alcohol abuse, who may also be a social worker or nurse, would be assigned as the case manager. He or she will link the man up with a physician for a thorough physical exam, a public health nurse to educate and supervise him in relation to eating habits, health maintenance, and abstinence, a social worker to develop a social support network, and a rehabilitation therapist to overcome the physical disabilities associated with chronic alcohol abuse. He may also be referred to an agency-sponsored AA group.

Case managers are also used in smaller agencies where they have to network among the staff members of other programs. Obviously, this leads to problems of ultimate case responsibility and "turf" issues, but it can be done. In fact, even large human service organizations sometimes have case managers who primarily serve as referral agents to other programs. Thus, if the girl presented herself at a small family planning clinic instead of a large community mental health center, the case manager's role would become one of linking her up to a private-practice psychologist for individual or family psychotherapy, as well as a school counselor or nurse to help the girl continue in school.

A word of caution is in order. Case management reached its peak in the late 1970s as a means of coordinating professional resources so that there would be less waste and overlap, and so that clients would receive all the diverse help that they need. Instead, research was found that this approach may only be adding an unnecessary bureaucratic layer that only makes service provision less efficient and more costly. Only careful planning with a clear recognition of the potential waste and pitfalls of case management can minimize its potentially harmful effects.

CASE MANAGEMENT EXERCISE

What is a fairly typical case in your agency? If yours is a direct service agency for individual clients, what is the most common cluster of problems and who else could help? Specifically, write down answers to the following questions:

(A) What is the most common problem or diagnosis in your agency?

(B) Describe a typical client with this problem and add two other problems or diagnoses that might typically also be involved. What sex, age, marital status, employment status, and so forth would this client have?

(C) What other professionals might be able to help this person? Include those whom you have only rarely, if ever, used for referrals. Be imaginative and ask others in your agency for suggestions.

(D) For each of the professionals listed above, answer the following questions:

 (1) Exactly how could they help?
 (2) Why would they help? Consider not only their agency's goals, but also political, economic, and personal considerations in relation to you, your own agency, and the community.
 (3) Why would they *not* help? Consider the same issues as above and include any obstacles standing in your way or their way with regard to developing case management linkages.

HUMAN SERVICE NETWORKS

A human service organization network is an ongoing, coordinated system of leaders of health, mental health, and social service agencies. It either meets as a group on a monthly basis or works through an information and referral agency to deal with problems pertinent to all the agencies, such as funding issues, legislation, community changes, "turf" or territorial issues among themselves, and the possibility of joint or shared resources and projects. The potential problems and difficulties related to developing and maintaining these networks are many, but let us first answer two questions: "What can they do?" and "How can they be started?"

What can human service organization networks do? They can minimize the waste of valuable professional resources by cutting back on the duplication of services. Most professionals are acutely aware of the fact that a minority of their clients are being seen by other professionals for virtually the same problem. The emphasis and even the goals of the intervention may be quite different, depending on whether a client is seen by a social worker, welfare worker, or lawyer, but the problem is the same.

For instance, a 19-year-old welfare recipient who is recently separated and the mother of a two-year-old could go to a number of sources for help in considering a divorce. A social worker would probably help this young woman with some problem-solving to establish whether a divorce is in her best interests and then proceed to establish tasks collaboratively in order to achieve this goal. A sensitive and well-trained lawyer or welfare worker might do the same thing but would then perform other tasks for which he or she is qualified. If a divorce were in the woman's best interests, a lawyer would then proceed to draw up the divorce papers, establish a court time, contact the husband or his attorney about the proceedings, and advise the woman about protecting her assets in any jointly owned property. Under the same circumstances, a welfare worker would develop a plan to maintain a sufficient income for the woman and her child and at least temporarily assign full custody of the child to the mother.

Without the coordination of a human service organization network, this woman could have gone to all three of these staffs and received either varying or even conflicting advice, thus adding to her burden. Based on the functioning of a Human Service Organization Network, the woman would have been referred to a social worker first, who would have helped her to clearly define the problem and the resultant goals and tasks. The social worker would then have referred the woman to a welfare worker after clearly defining and delineating the problem of financial resources and custody. The welfare worker would have then sent her to a lawyer for the necessary paperwork (which could be done by a paralegal or clerk) and for legal consultation regarding divorce proceedings.

Human service organization networks can be structured in one of two ways in order to use a community's professional resources most efficiently. They can either function as a committee or through a centralized clearinghouse.

The committee structure is a system in which the leaders of their authorized delegates serve in an ongoing group to manage and coordinate human services. Furthermore, where legislation arises that may have an impact on their community or their services, they would jointly discuss its impact. They may also proactively merge certain resources in order to develop proposals or establish needed services. Primarily, however, they would meet to clarify their varying areas of expertise.

Typically, such a network would consist of the leaders of agencies such as the community mental health center, Catholic, Jewish, and/or Lutheran social services, a family and children's social service agency, the state or county welfare department, a hospital with perhaps the department directors of social services, psychiatry, or nursing, the police department, and members of the clergy. The size should be kept between ten and twenty in order to develop and maintain some group dynamics that can foster better relationships. The meeting place can either be rotated among members on a monthly basis or kept at one facility that is "neutral" or nonthreatening (that is, not in competition for funds or clients). A city hall, public recreation building, or church may well serve the purpose. Ideally, the network would meet in a comfortable conference room around a table so that people could have eye-to-eye contact and could meet as peers.

The agenda for these networks varies, but when they are being started it is helpful to devote the first few sessions to a clarrification of the purpose of the human service organization network. In order to meet the network's goals, the member organizations should begin by sharing with each other all printed information about their agencies' organization, purposes, funding sources, and a description of their caseload size and presenting problems. This information need not be explicit. For instance, an agency may prefer to keep the name of a foundation secret if they fear competition from other member agencies, and may simply indicate a certain number of dollars from a private foundation. Also, agencies must protect the privacy and confidentiality of their cases.

Such basic guidelines may seem obvious, but I have been a member of two vastly different networks where even this much sharing of information was problematic. In one network in Michigan, the director of one program would not share any fiscal information. This was accepted by the other members, but it eventually became evident that her fear was not of the other agencies knowing the specifics of her funds, but rather of another program that was technically a part of the same organization as hers. She did not want the other department head in her own agency to know about her funds.

At the other end of this spectrum, I was a member of another network on an Indian reservation where an agency director shared far too much. At the second meeting of this network, a welfare worker from the Bureau of Indian Affairs carried in lists of the names, addresses, demographic data, and presenting problems for the agency. Most network members only need to have aggregate data and the types of problems that they treat. Greater levels of specificity are only used when a client has granted permission and when two or more agencies are using a case management approach to help a client.

This committee type of Human Service Organization Network facilitates the efficient use of services because the members of the committee share information about each other with their staff. In this way, the staff members of each agency learn when and how to refer cases to each other. Furthermore, the existence of the committee and the development of lines of communication legitimize and support these referrals. The committee's existence implicitly and explicitly indicates that agency staff should refer cases back and forth and help each other to serve the community. As time goes on, personal relationships and trust between staff members of different agencies develop, and the efficiency of the referral system is strengthened even more.

Coordination and linkages among human service organizations have been successfully performed for years at many levels. However, the term "networking" is rarely applied to the process in the organizational research and literature because the concept is still relatively new and because the focus of this body of knowledge tends to be on the sharing and linking of resources rather than on how some of these linkages are made or how decisions concerning these linkages begin a chain reaction or establish multiple and often diverse effects. Research has found that at different levels of a human service organization, all of which perform different functions, there also exist different types of linking needs (Gans and Horton, 1975).

These organizational linkages can be supported and encouraged by various networking efforts. Whether this is referred to as "integrating linkages" (Gans and Horton, 1975) or "linking program resources" (Lauffer, 1982), the purpose is to establish and support multiple connections and chain reactions. However, since organizations require the stratification and separation of certain functions (providing direct client services, accounting, developing funding sources, and so forth), different types of networking among organizations must be organized in different ways.

For instance, Lauffer (1982) identified six mechanisms that link agencies programmatically: case conferences, ad hoc case coordination, case management, joint intake screening and referral, information exchanges, and joint projects. However, staff linkages are also encouraged without establishing joint projects whenever a staff member is out-stationed from one agency to another; one agency lends a staff member to another; agencies assign their staff to liaison teams; agencies agree that one agency will be given responsibility for the screening and placement of staff; or several agencies engage in collaborative training and staff development efforts. At the more purely administrative level, such exchanges are fostered and networks developed through administrators providing or receiving technical assistance and consultation; joint establishing of standards or guidelines for practice with families and with children; developing integrated sets of procedures that facilitate other exchanges; joint public relations, publicity, or community education efforts; the sharing of facilities or equipment; and finally, joint evaluation.

Human Service Organizations can be started by any fairly central or well-connected leader of an agency. He or she does not have to be the director of the agency, although in most instances that is preferable. Furthermore, he or she does not have to be with the most "powerful" or largest agency in the community. In fact, other agencies become suspicious when either a very large or an apparently very aggressive agency establishes such a network leadership role for itself.

There are four issues that must be considered throughout the process of networking for a committee structure of a human service organization network. These are territory, status, power, and trust.

Every agency has defined for itself a certain geographical as well as problem territory. The geographical limits tend to be clearly defined by most organizations. For instance, public agencies funded by a county or municipal government are obviously required to stay within their county or city. Generally, federally funded programs must define a catchment area or geographic boundary in order to receive funds. Church-related organizations will be defined on the basis of the boundaries of the parish, congregation, or diocese. While there is inevitably overlap and even conflict over geographic territory, it can often be worked out by mutual agreement and tends to be a more clear-cut and manageable dispute than that of "problem" territory.

Problem territory refers to the agreement on the part of certain programs that one agency has precedence over others with regard to certain types of problems elicited by clients. This is rarely a simple task. Professionals tend to view many more people as having the particular problems that they treat than do others. For instance, an unemployed, depressed, alcoholic, single-parent woman could very easily be viewed by at least four separate agencies as being *their* client. Who is to decide whether vocational rehabilitation, the community mental health center, the hospital's outpatient alcoholism unit, or the Family and Children's Social Service worker should first see the woman? Because of the tremendous diversity in client problems, as well as the diversity of various programs' resources based on location, funding, expertise, and other factors, this issue has to be worked out among committee network members—not on a case-by-case basis, but on the basis of general guidelines. Thus, the committee network members may agree among themselves that unless a client is clinically depressed (according to the definition wherein the client must have a sleep disorder, loss or gain of weight, lethargy, and at least occasional outbreaks of crying or suicidal ideation), he or she should be seen at the community mental health center. Ultimately, a very rough list of critical problems and needs would be developed that could be disseminated among the staff members of all the network organizations, a list that would indicate both the priorities of agencies and their presenting problems. In other words, agencies would have to say: "These are the two or three types of client problems that we must see and accept primary responsibility for."

Status and interprofessional competition is another issue in social services and mental health which is an embarrassing reality of everyday professional life. People tend to define status on the basis of their own idiosyncratic set of criteria, and thus it becomes confusing to all network members, none of whom share the same criteria. Medical doctors seem particularly prone to assume leadership positions of networks before others have granted them that authority. Other professionals can be equally insensitive and ill advised in presuming that either they or their organizations have more or less status based on the type of degree they hold, or on their organization's size or funds. Status and respect have to be earned in the network. In fact, in instances where networks formalize their structure and actually elect a leader, he or she is *not* usually the director of the biggest organization or the member with the most prestigious degree. Such factors can even be liabilities in a network such as this where coordination and management can be suspiciously viewed as competition and control.

Power in the network becomes an issue only in relation to the authority of network members to act. Human Service Organization Network members must be in a position of authority within their own organizations or their clout and credibility within the networks could diminish. Ultimately, the impact of the whole network could be weakened if it consisted of those without authority. A Human Service Organization Network must include directors of major agencies, or at least their immediate subordinates in the case of very large agencies. Direct service staff who cannot speak authoritatively about the possibility of reallocating their agency's resources should not be members.

One of the more blatant and sadly humorous maneuvers to undermine a network that I have ever seen happened in relation to this issue. A program director I knew in Michigan had been attending the sessions regularly but was uncharacteristically silent at them and, I later realized, quite threatened by the network's existence. She was required to come for political reasons, but after one meeting in which all of the network members agreed to refer a certain type of client to an agency other than hers, even though her agency was peripherally involved in that area, she decided to seek revenge. At the next monthly network meeting, she sent a substitute—not her assistant director, or even her director of clinical services, but a new, first-year graduate student from the School of Social Work!

In order for a network to coordinate and manage its services, members must be in a position to allocate their agency's resources. The representative has to be either the director or another high-level person who will not be countermanded from above.

Finally, perhaps the most significant factor in developing a successful Human Service Organization Network is the relatively elusive element of trust. A network such as this does, in fact, bring together agencies that more often view each other as competitors than allies. This viewpoint has to be reversed.

A network with this committee structure is in fact a group and, therefore, will be affected by small-group dynamics. As such, we know that interaction and thus relationships can be increased and developed through providing a consistent and comfortable meeting place where participants can see and hear each other. Furthermore, if a group leader or networker can model and develop an atmosphere within the network wherein members can openly and honestly air their opinions and concerns, the network is far more likely to succeed.

For instance, if the networker and potential leader or developer of this network modeled certain risk-taking behavior, others might follow suit. This does not mean that one must admit publicly all of one's agency's flaws, but it may help to let other agencies know what types of clients one's agency is currently serving whom others might better serve. Or, if other agency staff have been erroneously referring a certain type of client to an agency that do not, in fact, have staff with the necessary type of expertise, the staff may suggest future referrals to another network member agency. Obviously, this method cannot be used to "dump" unwanted clients, but it can be used as a way of modeling to get other network members to do the same.

Other ways of developing trust within the committee network include:

(1) supporting positive, constructive statements by other members;
(2) discouraging undermining of the network by constructively, positively, but firmly confronting members who are hurting the network;
(3) providing one's own agency's resources, such as staff, telephones, and mailing, to continue the work of the network;
(4) consistently attending meetings, and following up absences by others with phone calls;
(5) developing joint grant proposals and research projects;
(6) developing joint lobbying efforts on behalf of any network member agency, even where the results do not directly affect one's own agency or clients;
(7) develop and support subcommittees that report back to the network regarding common problems of the community and ways of jointly meeting community needs.

Other than the committee, a second way of structuring human service organization networks is through a clearinghouse or information and referral (I&R) service. An I&R agency is often funded by United Way or a similarly donated public trust fund. Such an agency provides no direct service or counseling to anyone, but simply refers the public and professionals to the most appropriate resource in the community.

I have worked closely for the past few years with the Information and Volunteer Service (IVS) agency for Pittsburgh and the surrounding area. It serves this I&R function in a variety of ways. Primarily, it serves as the repository of information on all health, mental health, and social service agencies in and around the city. All of this information is stored in its computer and updated periodically. When the public or professionals call the agency to ask where to receive certain services, they are informed by staff members precisely where to go and what optional services they have. The agency also has a 24-hour hotline that serves the public, but it also brings in needed extra money for the agency by providing evening coverage for local community mental health programs. The IVS staff screen clients for the community mental health center staff so that the staff at the five centers do not all have to be available constantly.

This clearinghouse or the I&R type of Human Service Organization Network can also help by publishing a list or directory of services in the community. In Pittsburgh, IVS publishes the "Where To Turn" directory of every conceivable type of agency and human service. It is sold at cost to agencies throughout the area, and those who purchase it are sent periodical updates. A network such as this must be established as an independent organization under United Way or a Health and Welfare Planning Council.

The committee-type network takes some very different skills to get started.

Linkages among organizations can be more easily developed and continued under certain circumstances (Feldman, 1976; Boys, 1982). When organizations have common goals and objectives, as well as written agreements clearly specifying their respective roles, this diminishes the likelihood of conflict. Also, specific staff from member agencies need to be assigned and must be willing to commit time and effort to developing good work relationships. Joint efforts in collecting data useful to the community is also helpful, particularly when these can then provide feedback to the programs and community leaders involved. Two final issues that seem to encourage networking among organizations include the use of citizens in bridging conflicts and the use of the great motivator—money.

The issue of the problems and obstacles related to organizational networking that seem particularly relevant to the clearinghouse model were addressed by Rossi et al. (1982) along with some suggestions for overcoming them. They see five obstacles to such coordination:

(1) *crisis operation*—the perception within agencies that they are barely keeping their heads above water and that they are therefore unable to consider rationally alternative approaches to service delivery, even though this is needed to break their cycle of crisis operation;
(2) *inflexibility*—intolerance for deviating from regular agency policy;
(3) *turfsmanship*—according to Rossi et al., the belief that additional "turf," clients, or responsibilities are needed to ensure agency survival, a belief that leads to competitiveness;
(4) *bureaucracy*—the red tape and extra time required to move decisions through an administrative hierarchy;
(5) *politics*—the problems related to the fact that priorities are imposed by federal, state, and local political issues, and that these conflict at times.

How do the authors suggest dealing with these obstacles? By doing the following:

(1) recognize their existence;
(2) focus attention on the overriding objective, the greater good;
(3) identify key allies; and
(4) make use of a reward structure that fosters interagency coordination instead of allowing a system that works against it.

Human Service Organization Networks, as well as case management networks, are both potential ways of saving valuable human resources.

Both involve planning and an awareness of potential problems. However, if carefully planned and executed, the networks will minimize the wasteful overlap of services, increase cooperation among agencies and their staff, minimize harmful and destructive competition among programs, and ultimately increase significantly the combined capacity of agencies to gather new resources.

REFERENCES

BOYS, G. A. (1982) "Community care for the mentally disabled: practical steps toward interorganizational linkages." Presented at the National Council of Community Mental Health Centers, New York, March 12.

CURTIS, W. R. (1981) Managing Human Services with Less: New Strategies for Local Leaders. Human Services Monograph Series, Project Share, No. 26.

FELDMAN, S. (1976) "Mental health under the umbrella." Hospital and Community Psychiatry 27 (January): 25-29.

GANS, S. P. and G. T. HORTON (1975) Integration of Human Services. New York: Praeger.

LAUFFER, A. (1982) Getting the Resources You Need. Beverly Hills, CA: Sage.

ROSSI, R. J., K. J. GILMARTIN, and C. W. DAYTON (1982) Agencies Working Together: A Guide to Coordination and Planning. Beverly Hills, CA: Sage.

Chapter 7

NETWORKING WITH COMMUNITIES

Communities are composed of networks, and networks are composed of people helping each other. When these natural helping networks are linked together, or at least when the potential exists within a community to link them up in order to help people, the social fabric of a community is strengthened and the quality of life in that community enhanced.

Recent researchers and theorists in the field of community psychology and community organization have recognized the significance of networks within communities (Warren, 1981; Froland et al., 1981; Maguire and Biegel, 1982; Garbarino and Stocking, 1980; Maguire, 1983; Naperstek et al., 1982; Cunningham and Kotler, 1983). By conceptualizing and analyzing communities on the basis of their network configurations, community researchers and theorists have not only begun a whole new era, with its accompanying new and exciting possibilities, but they have found a methodological tool that is clearly a good "fit" in this field. It is not surprising that the methodology is one that came initially from anthropology, a social science that is respected for its sensitive and in-depth, unobtrusive analysis of cultures and the patterns of interaction and influence among group members. We can only hope that those of us in other fields who have gained from the tremendous methodological boost that network analysis has given us will also appreciate the anthropologists' keen recognition of the value of non-interference where there is a danger of undermining natural supports.

Communities have relatively little to do with geographic boundaries and a great deal to do with multiple linkages and chain reactions. Contrary to what was thought only a few short years ago, communities are also networks. They are natural helping networks of relatives, friends, neighbors, co-workers, gatekeepers, politicians, teachers, clergy, and professionals of every type. One can understand and appropriately help communities when one recognizes what these networks are, how they work, and what can and cannot be done with them.

In reference to communities, there are two basic types of networks that are relevant. The first of these is the social network anchored on the basis of individuals. That type of network was rather extensively considered in the earlier chapters of this book. It was established that the social networks of individuals help in a wide variety of ways and that there is a correlation between several mental health or quality-of-life indicators and such factors as the size, density, and utilization of one's network.

Social network analyses are significant to community theorists partly because of their linkage or lack of linkage with the other type of network—natural helping networks. Individuals are connected to many different networks. Outside of their own inner circle of close friends and relatives, they are frequently either directly or indirectly linked to certain natural helping networks as well. While some theorists see both of these types of networks as being natural helping networks (Warren, 1981), others prefer to differentiate between the two, preferring to reserve the name "natural helping networks" for those not anchored with individuals, but rather on problems or issues (Collins and Pancoast, 1976).

Networking strategies within communities usually involve techniques that use a consultation or support approach to various "problem-anchored helping networks" (PAHNs), as Warren (1981) calls them, or that identify key community leaders who are gatekeepers for or central to natural helping networks within communities.

Community networking involves a very similar process to networking with organizations, except that natural community support systems and networks are used more than formal organizations and professionals.

Knowledge and conceptualizations about communities, what they are and what they do, have all gone through radical revisions recently. Advances in methods such as network analysis and findings regarding social support have all culminated in a new understanding of communities as a system of problem-solving networks and natural helping networks. There are clearly a variety of networks within communities that serve the needs of their inhabitants. Networkers need to be able to recognize those networks and link them up with community people or with each other to serve as a support system.

In the last chapter, we examined networking with professionals, managing cases, and also how to set up a system of professional organizations and agencies to establish a human service network. In this chapter we will see how to develop natural helping networks within communities and how to use nonprofessional key leaders and gatekeepers as the primary focus, with professionals serving in an advisory and support role.

Natural helping networks develop spontaneously, and neither their structure nor their process should be undermined by obtrusive interventions by professionals. Yet social workers can aid their communities by identifying these natural helping networks and by helping them to develop their linkages and coordinate their chain reactions. Networkers need to assist in the empowerment of the community.

NETWORKING FOR COMMUNITY EMPOWERMENT

An exciting and highly effective method of networking in communities has been developed in recent years. It is based on the assumption that most communities already have tremendous resources that are overlooked and sometimes even undermined by professionals working in communities. The community mental health empowerment model (Biegel and Naparstek, 1982; Naparstek et al., 1982; Fields, 1980) emphasizes the strengths of neighborhoods and is designed to link together a neighborhood's own support system and a professional network.

To network in communities, using the community empowerment approach, one needs to keep several objectives in mind. One is to create an awareness on the part of neighborhood residents of the neighborhood's own strengths, as well as its needs. One needs to work through existing organizations and place the sponsorship and ownership of the program clearly with the community. To help the residents become aware of and involved with their own resources, it helps to have the community residents gather data and conduct surveys for and by themselves. One also needs to develop a task force of community residents, natural helpers, clergy, local union officials, presidents of ethnic organizations and social clubs, and other gatekeepers to meet on an ongoing basis in order to examine and deal with problems that they feel exist in their own community. When "outside experts" come into a community and define a problem such as drug abuse and then begin to rectify the problem, community residents are likely to see it as an attack, rather than a helpful and constructive act. Community networking has legitimacy within the community only when it is carried out by the residents of a neighborhood and their own friends and neighbors.

The second objective is to strengthen the neighborhood lay helping network. While we know that some community networks exist around specific problems (Warren, 1981) or specific resource needs (Collins and Pancoast, 1976), most of the natural helpers within communities do not know each other and do not constitute a preexisting network (Naparstek et al., 1982). Networkers need to help community gatekeepers such as priests, pharmacists, teachers, and community leaders to identify the natural helpers and then link them up with the task force or committees of community leaders. These natural helpers can be invaluable resources for a community and will add strength and legitimacy to one's efforts, though they frequently avoid involvement with professionals. Furthermore, they do not see themselves as providing a "service," as professionals do, nor do they often even see themselves as helpers. They are simply good neighbors and friends to people who need help. They have to be approached cautiously and slowly, or else one could undermine their work. In some instances, it may be sufficient for them to know of the existence of your efforts to develop committees and networks of community residents, gatekeepers, and professionals. They may prefer not to be visible, active members of the task force or committees, preferring to assist on an "as needed" basis when asked simply to help out a neighbor.

The third objective is to help strengthen the professional helping network. In this model by Naparstek et al. (1982), one needs to organize professionals who work in a community into Professional Advisory Committees (PAC). These PACs are composed of professionals who work in the local social service agencies, schools, drug or alcohol abuse programs, hospitals, community mental health centers, child guidance clinics, nursing homes, or courts. One may find in developing these PACs that many of the people do not know one another. PACs, which are similar to the Human Service Networks described earlier, are composed only of professionals and are only advisory in nature. It is the community leaders and their task force who must take the lead in the community.

The next objective is to link the task force with a PAC. In this model, the task force invited professionals to join them on certain committees. While the PAC and the task force kept their separate meetings and agendas, they developed a partnership and worked collaboratively on many projects. This linkage needs to be developed and encouraged, or else the two systems could become competitive with each other.

The last objective in this community networking approach, which stresses community empowerment, is to link the lay and professional helping networks and the macrosystem. In other words, one must get the task force, the PACs, and any community committees to work together on projects that can help the community in relation to the rest of society. For instance, the two groups might agree to write a grant proposal together that would provide transportation for the elderly or a recreation center for teenagers. Or they may decide to send a delegation to their state capital to lobby for a new school or an addition to the local hospital. When community leaders and professional leaders combine forces on projects that benefit an area, they tend to complement each other. Funding sources such as foundations and the government increasingly recognize the need for collaborative efforts on the part of professionals, who have the credentials and technical expertise to carry out projects, and the local residents and leaders, who will see that a project deals appropriately with a real need. Working together helps to bring these two groups closer and effectively demonstrates networking in action.

BEGINNING THE PROCESS

In the community empowerment model, we saw an example of an outside expert coming into a community and carefully and sensitively helping people to analyze and use their own community networks and resources. However, it is probably more likely to be a social worker or nurse or psychologist who is concerned about networking in the community in which he or she already works and perhaps lives. Where does this person begin?

Getting back to my original definition of networking, one can begin by using one's own multiple linkages to develop chain reactions. In other words, where a problem exists or a crisis develops, one contacts one's own network of fellow professionals and community leaders and has them get in touch with others with resources. Finally, all meet and decide on a plan of coordinated action.

This process has been studied and tested in numerous cities throughout the country by Cunningham and Kotler (1983) who list fourteen organizing steps for building a new neighborhood organization. These are:

(1) A crisis or a significant problem exists in the community or a community organizer deliberately provokes some people.
(2) A group or network of concerned people meet together.
(3) This network or cadre defines the problem more clearly and begins to work on it.
(4) This network links up with others as the issue attracts interest.
(5) The network and its followers achieve some success on the issue and seek other outside allies, if needed.
(6) The network and others establish a permanent committee or organization out of existing organizations or individual members.
(7) The new organization evolves a strategy to get things done by pressuring government or others, by providing services to community residents, or perhaps both.
(8) The new organization becomes involved with other issues of concern to the community, thus developing a power base using cooperation, campaigning, and/or confrontation, as appropriate.

(9) New members are trained to be more effective.
(10) Regular channels of communication are formed among members and to the public.
(11) A stable source of income is developed, but no more than is necessary.
(12) The organization networks with other organizations to form alliances.
(13) Evaluation is begun and routinely used.
(14) Recruiting new members and dealing with new issues goes on as the organization grows and develops.

These same steps are routinely used for new organizations, committees of concerned community leaders, PACs, community task forces, and Human Service Networks. The central idea is still linking people up with people who know and care about issues and problems in the community and who are willing and able to do something about them.

My experience has been that the most successful networking in communities develops from small networks of people who know each other, have a good degree of trust, and are effective in following through with commitments. These then grow and evolve into other types of networks or committees, or even whole new agencies. The emphasis in this process has to be on growth and change, not in merely developing a static organization that will control resources.

I was involved in a community networking example in Michigan where the director of a community mental health center became very concerned about the "dumping" of former psychiatric patients into her catchment area. She called the directors of three other mental health-related agencies, who in turn called the mayor's office, the state hospital, four clergy, two community organization directors, a self-help group leader, and the head of the city's housing office. This interesting conglomeration of people met within ten days of the initial call. Few of these people knew each other directly, although all of them seemed to know at least two or three others and indirectly knew of at least another two. At the first session, after people introduced one another (although this was used only as an icebreaker, since the names, agency affiliations, and telephone numbers of everyone present were passed out along with the agenda), the discussion began. The representative from the state hospital was quite defensive and explained that they were trying their best to ease patients back into the community but felt little cooperation from anywhere else. He felt that neither family, neighbors, nor community groups such as those represented at the meeting were offering to help. Two of the mental health program directors indicated that they had frequently extended their agency's services to the hospital to help but invariably became lost in the process and felt that their recommendations were ignored. One clergyman said that he had formed a group of as many as forty of these former patients who met regularly at his church and shared coffee and talked with each other. The existence of this group came as a surprise to nearly all of the professionals, and only the leader of the self-help group was aware of its existence.

That first meeting of the network accomplished many things. It got the community leaders talking to each other, even though the discussion was initially characterized by defensiveness. It also made the members aware of what others were doing and not doing, and it made them more aware of each other's resources. The session also sensitized them to the existence of a problem of which all of them were aware but unsure of how to confront it. Finally, it got them to begin networking with each other by developing plans, sharing resources, and cooperating with regard to a common community problem.

The next few sessions were planning sessions in which each network member presented plans of action and specific ways in which their respective agencies could help. The membership of this particular network changed in size and membership and only lasted for about five months, but it was effective. A new multiple referral pattern was developed between the hospital and the other concerned programs. The animosity toward the hospital diminished considerably as others became aware of the hospital's problems and limitations, as well as its genuine concern for an orderly transition into the community.

EXERCISE

What problems exist in your own community which need attention? Who would you enlist to help you and how would you do it?

Based on your knowledge of your community, write the following exercise:

(1) Define a major community problem and describe it as specifically as possible.

(2) List the people whom you would contact to help you with this problem. Remember to include fellow professionals from a variety of agencies, the clergy, the leaders of unions or ethnic organizations, politicians, natural helpers, medical personnel, and any others from the formal or informal helping system who could be of help.

(3) Review your list and write down the types of resources each of these people might provide, as well as the potential obstacles each of them may meet from within their own agencies or support systems, from other

network members, or from other community people. Are there other limitations, such as funding or authority, that might develop for each of them?

(4) Specifically describe what you see as the best one or two ways to deal with the problem, taking into consideration any obstacles and limitations.

By organizing these concerns, names, resources, plans, and potential problems before convening the network, one can anticipate and therefore diminish the likelihood of certain problems developing. Community networking is, however, a fluid process and one must be ready for many changes and surprises with it. However, by going into it with a clear understanding of the problem and the people and other resources needed to overcome it, anyone can be a successful networker.

REFERENCES

BIEGEL, D. E. and A. NAPARSTEK (1982) Community Support Systems in Mental Health: Practice, Policy and Research. New York: Springer.
COLLINS, A. and D. PANCOAST (1976) Natural Helping Networks. Washington, DC: National Association of Social Workers.
CUNNINGHAM, J. V. and M. KOTLER (1983) Building Neighborhood Organizations. Notre Dame, IN: University of Notre Dame Press.
FIELDS, S. (1980) "Mental health networks: extending the community's circuits of care." Innovations 7 (Spring).
FROLAND, C., D. L. PANCOAST, N. J. CHAPMAN, and P. J. KIMBOKO (1981) Helping Networks and Human Services. Beverly Hills, CA: Sage.
GARBARINO, J. and S. H. STOCKING (1980) Protecting Children from Abuse and Neglect. San Francisco: Jossey-Bass.
MAGUIRE, L. (1983) "Networking for self-help: an empirically based guideline," in F. M. Cox et al. (eds.) Tactics and Techniques of Community Practice (2nd ed.). Itasca, IL: F. E. Peacock.
——— and D. E. BIEGEL (1982) "The use of networks in social welfare: jumping on the bandwagon," in Social Welfare Forum. New York: Columbia University Press.
NAPARSTEK, A., D. E. BIEGEL, and H. SPIRO (1982) Neighborhood Networks for Humane Mental Health Care. New York: Plenum.
WARREN, D. (1981) Helping Networks: How People Cope with Problems in the Urban Community. Notre Dame, IN: University of Notre Dame Press.

ABOUT THE AUTHOR

Lambert Maguire chairs the Interpersonal or Clinical area at the University of Pittsburgh's School of Social Work. He has a Ph.D. in both social work and psychology from the University of Michigan in Ann Arbor and is a graduate of the University of Chicago's School of Social Service Administration. He is a commissioned officer in the U.S. Public Health Service and has worked in community mental health centers in Ann Arbor and on the Pine Ridge Indian Reservation in South Dakota. Before coming to Pittsburgh he directed a treatment outcome research project funded by NIMH and currently directs a clinical training project that deals with social networks and community support systems.